The Piano Compendium

A Selection of Pieces for Piano

Book 4
Performance Pieces for Diplomas

KONSTANTINOS PAPATHEODOROU

Erebus Society

First published in Great Britain in 2018
Erebus Society

First Edition

Arrangement © Konstantinos Papatheodorou 2018
Cover © Constantin Vaughn 2018

ISBN 978-1-912461-09-7

www.erebussociety.com

TABLE OF CONTENTS

PERFORMANCE PIECES

Claude Debussy – Clair de Lune 3

Franz Liszt – Hungarian Rhapsody No 12 10

Franz Liszt - La Campanella - Grandes Etudes de Paganini No. 3 22

Franz Schubert – Wandered Fantasy in C Major, Opus 15 32

Frédéric François Chopin – Etude in C Minor, Opus 25, No 12 54

Frédéric François Chopin – Fantaisie Impromptu, Opus 66 60

Ludwig Van Beethoven – Opus No 13, "Pathetique" 70

Ludwig Van Beethoven – Sonata No 14, Opus 27, No 2 (Moonlight Sonata)...............101

Nikolai Andreyevich Rimsky-Korsakov – Flight of the Bumblebee.................120

Sergei Rachmaninoff - Prelude in D Minor, Opus 23, No 3 126

Performance Pieces

Clair de Lune

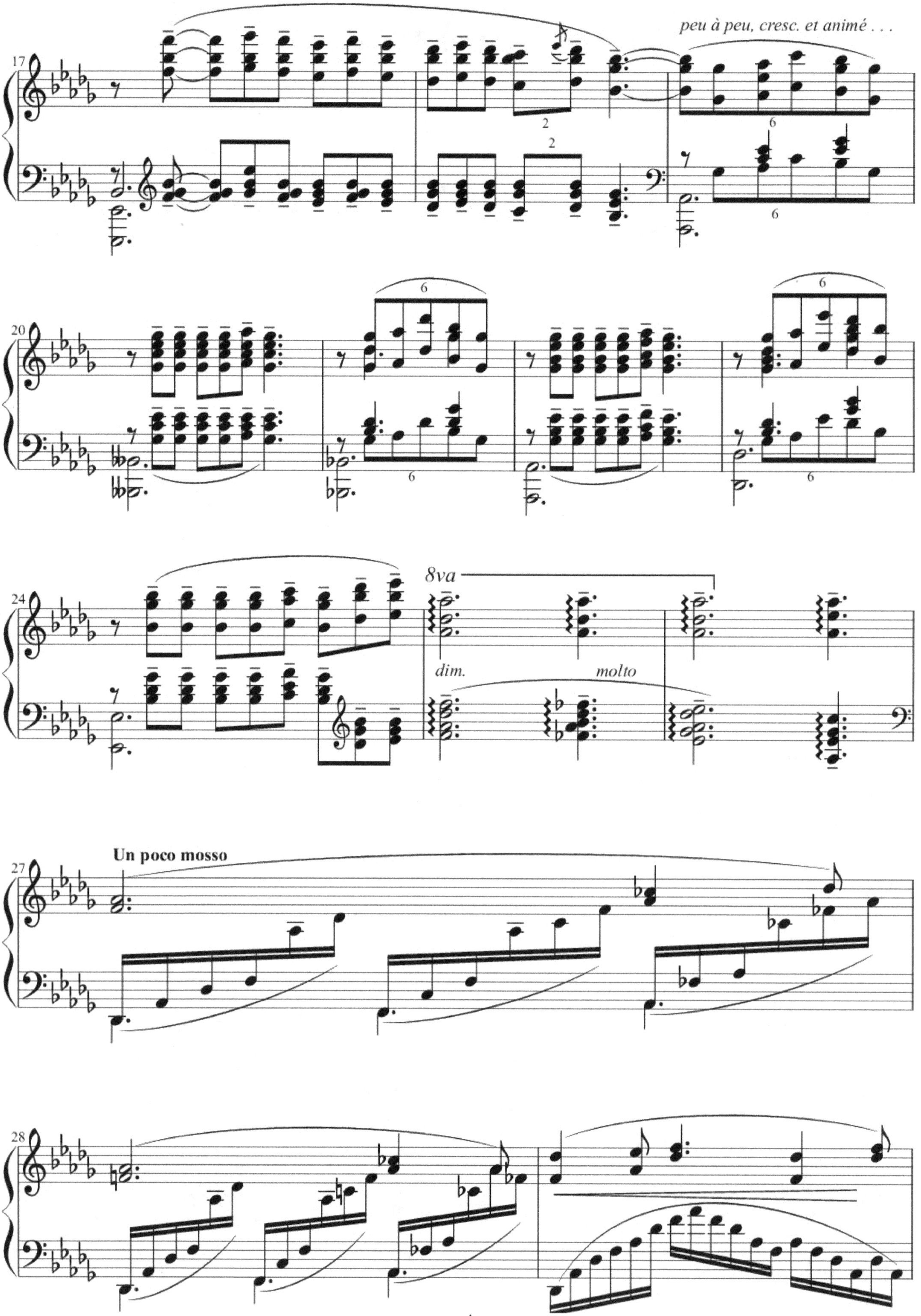
peu à peu, cresc. et animé . . .
8va
dim.
molto
Un poco mosso

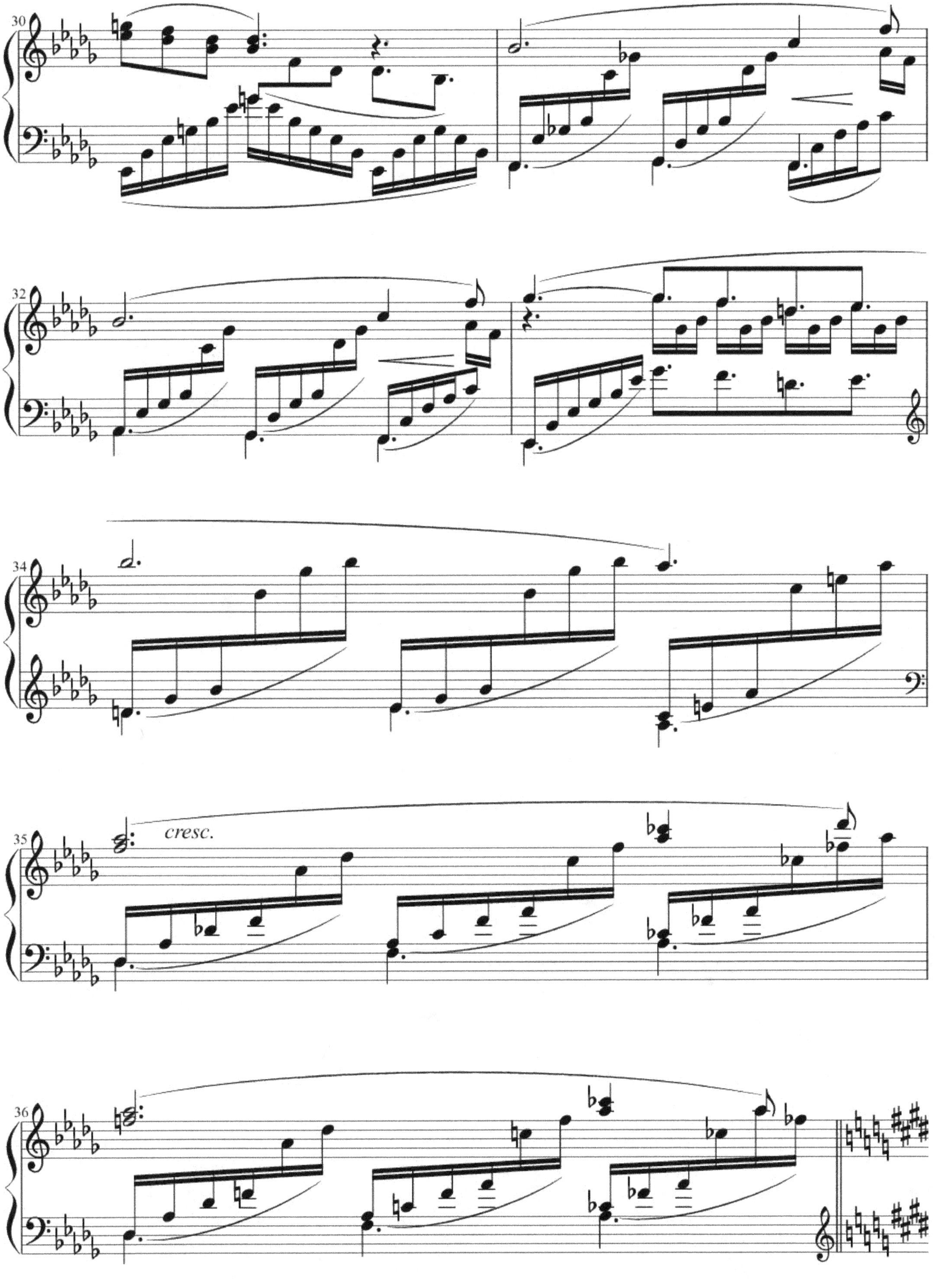
cresc.

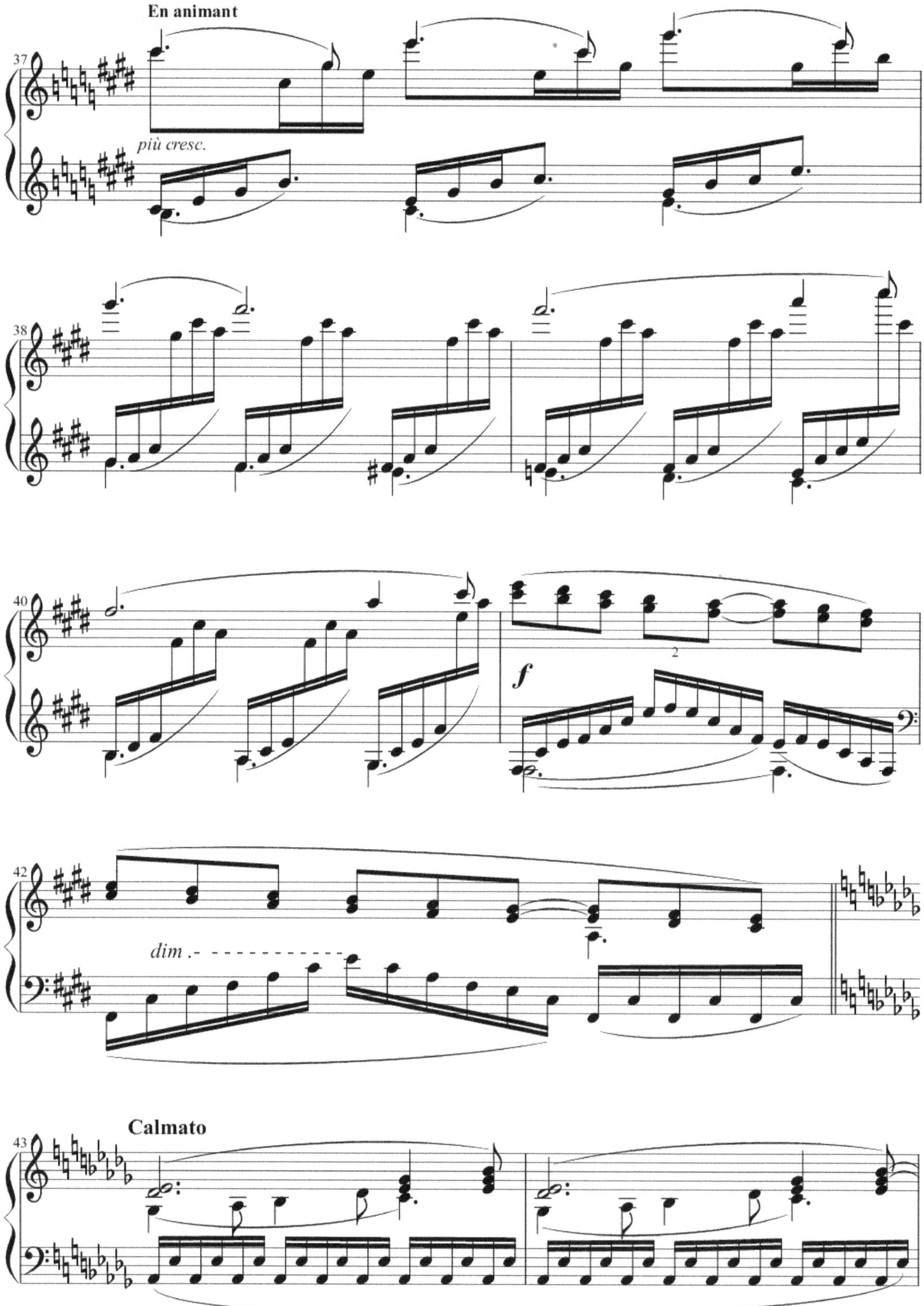

En animant
37
più cresc.
38
40
f
42
dim .-
43
Calmato

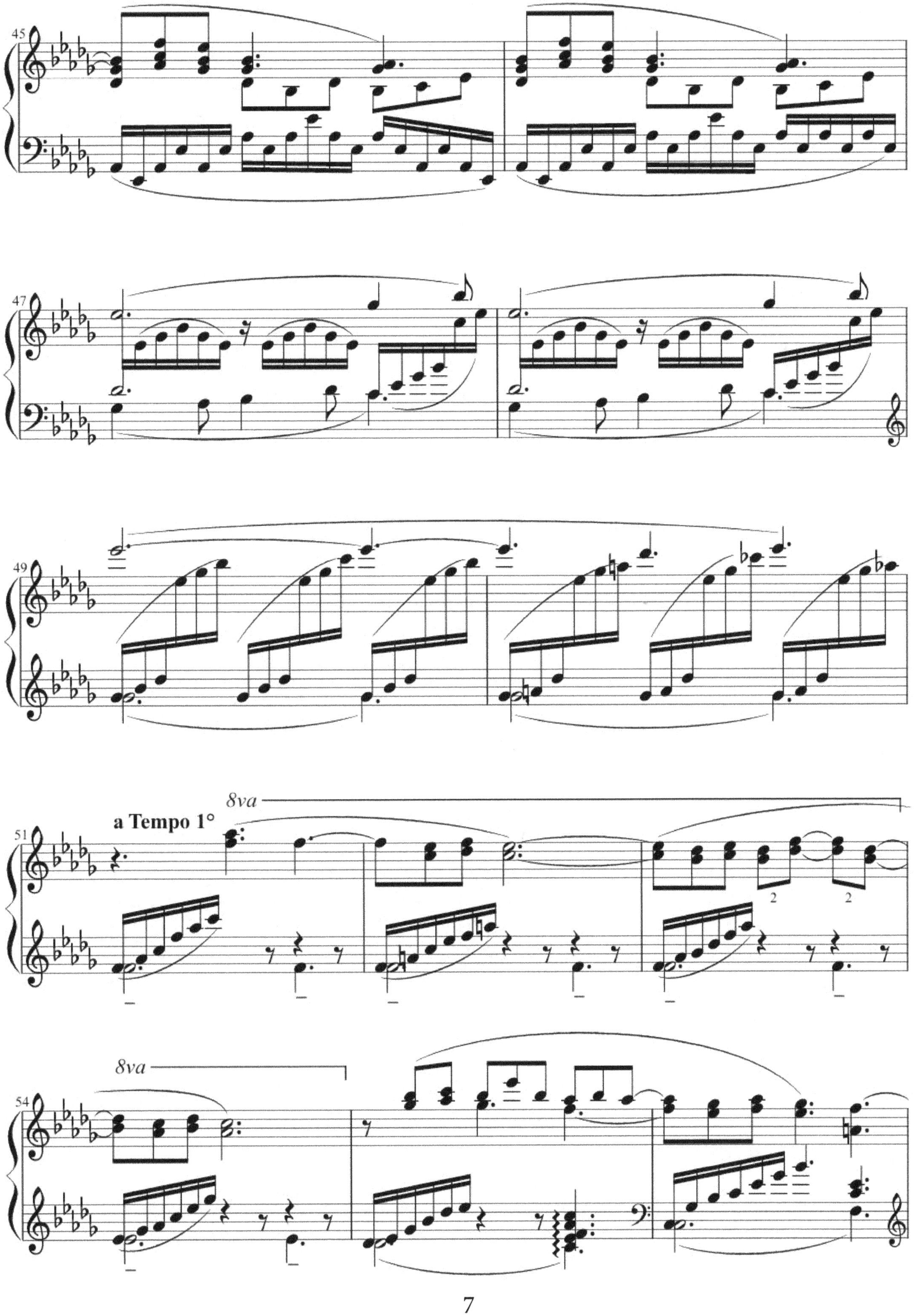
45
47
49
a Tempo 1°
8va
51
8va
54

morendo jusqu'à la fin

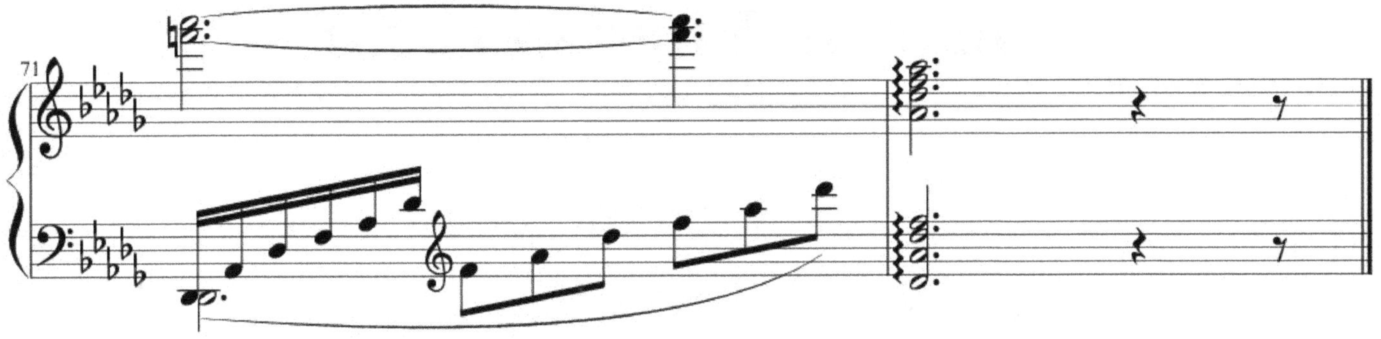
71

Hungarian Rhapsody No 12

Franz Liszt

string.
rall.
f
sf
rfz
Adagio
rinforz. assai
pause lunga
pesante
Un poco più lento
in tempo in libitum
espressivo
rit. a piacere
sfz
stretto
dolce.
A tempo
legato
pesante

rinforz
legato
rinforz
Sempre dolce, ma ben marcato in melodia
p
lungo trillo
longo trillo
sempre p capricciosamesamete
sempre pedal

66
8va
Un poco accal.
sempre p quasi campanelle
dim. non legato
sempre Pedal
71
78
cresc.
dim.
84
smorz.
ppp
dolce con grazia
90
rall.
95
Ritenuto il tempo sempre rubato
smorz.
dolce con grazia

100
8va
pp
riten.
e
smorz.
Ped.
104
Tempo I
tremolando
p
sotto voce
cresc. molto
8va
ff
9
coll'8vb
107
sotto voce
cresc. molto
8va
ff
9
coll'8vb
110
quasi marcia
ff
6
3
114
12
8va
sf
6
117
rinforz
8va
rinforz
8va
8va

120
8va
ff strepitoso.
Ped.
121
dim.
125
6
Allegretto giojoso
longo trillo
p
128
marcato il tema
rit.
135
ppp
pp
dolce.
grazioso.
139
coll'8va

147
coll'8va
8va
rit.
in tempo.
loco
p
155
cresc.
160
poco rall.
167
3
ppp
170
pp
p
175
Ped.

179
tr
6
8va
12
Ped.
181
8va
5
Ped.
182
8va
5
Ped.
183
p
p
Ped.
190
Ped.
194
8va
Ped.

197
cresc.
202
8va
206
p sempre vivace
210
sempre stacc.
217
222

224
8va
229
un poco marcato ma
sempre p
234
cresc.
237
240
f brioso
ff
Ped.
243

247
ff
accel.
cresc.
252
8va
rinforz. assai
il più presto possible
255
leggiero
258
8va
8va
261
264
8va
cresc.

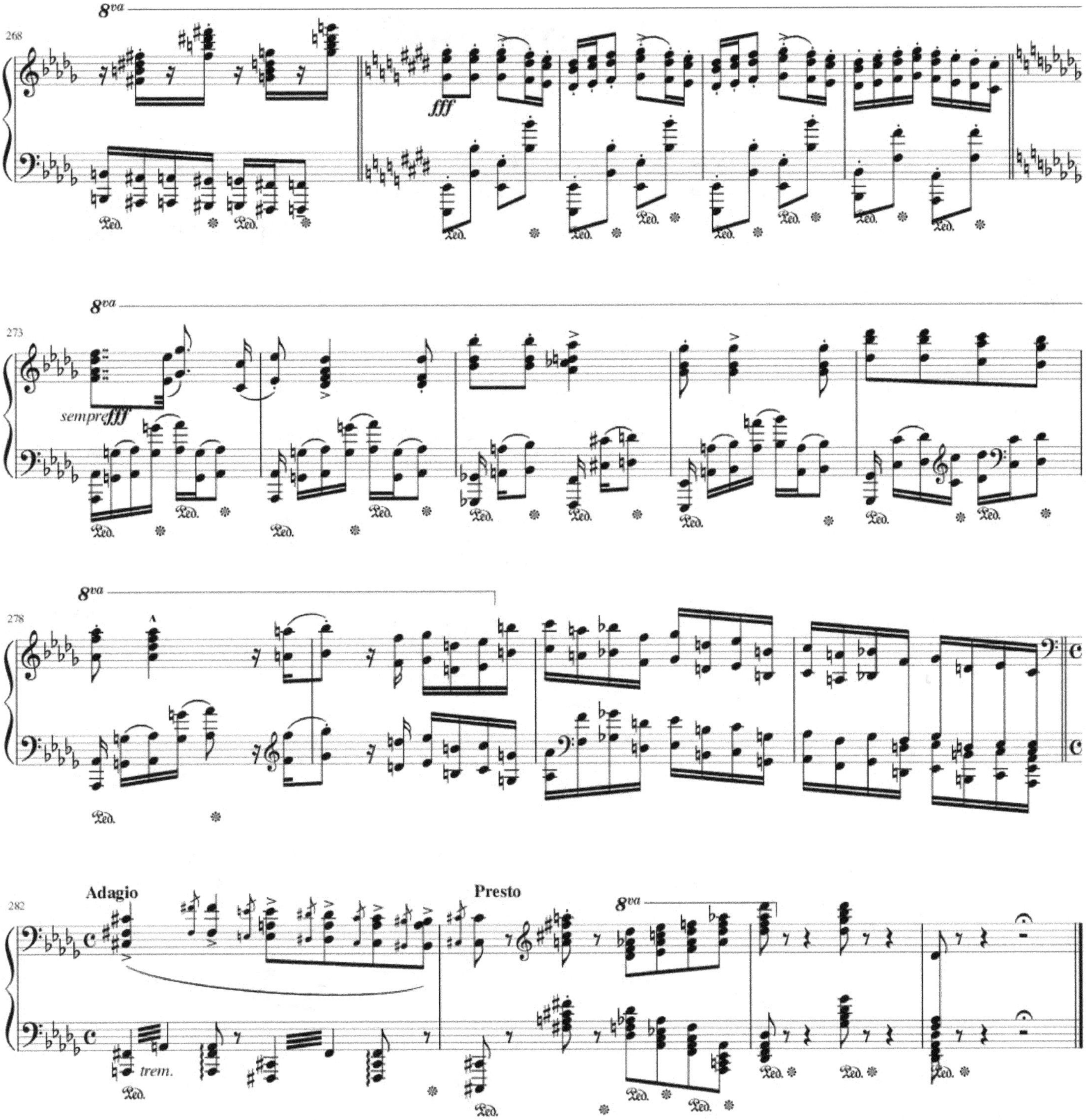
8va
268
fff
Ped.
273
sempre fff
278
282
Adagio
Presto
trem.

La Campanella
Grandes Etudes de Paganini No. 3

Franz Liszt

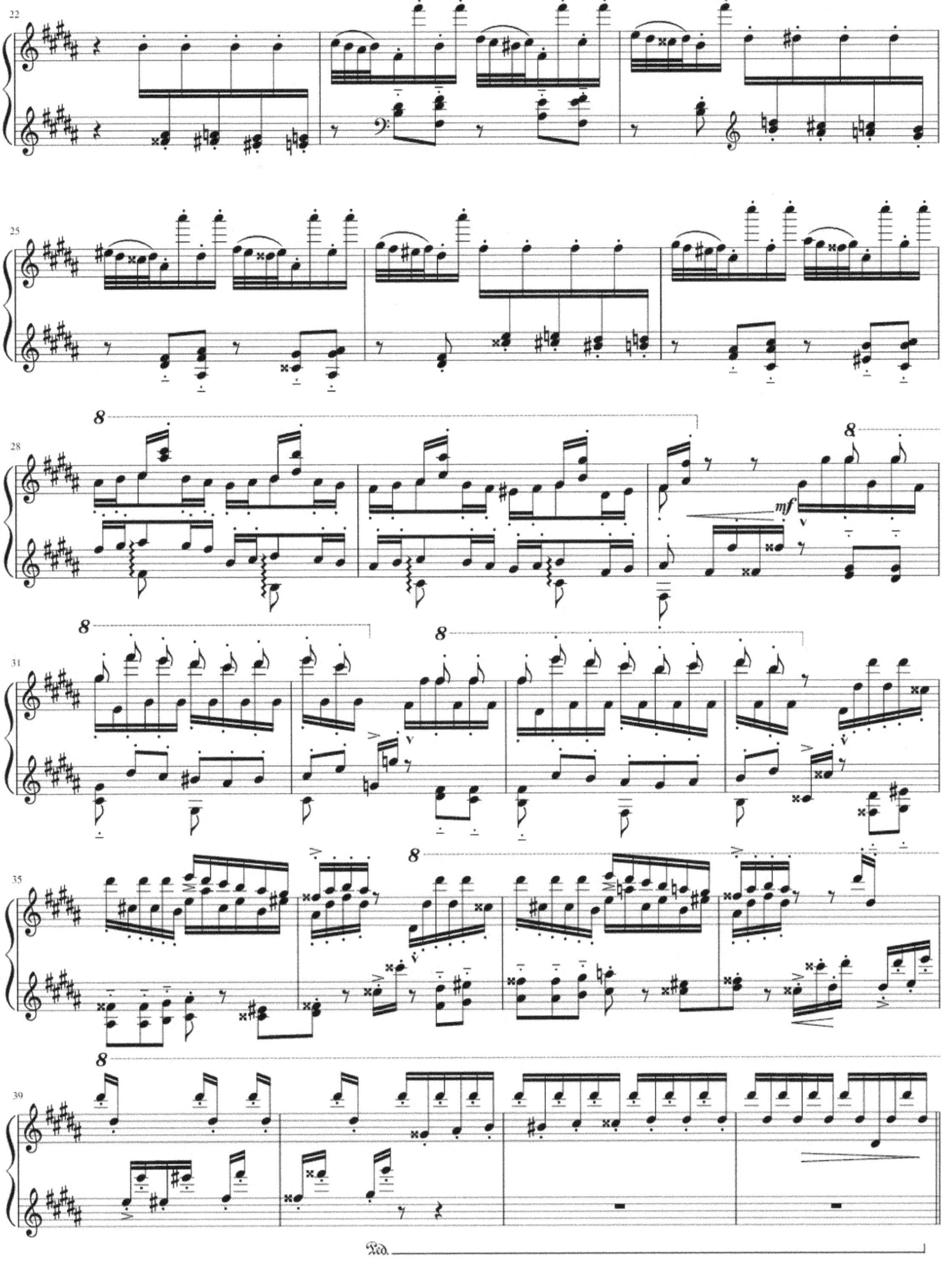
22
25
28
8
mf
31
8
35
39
Ped.

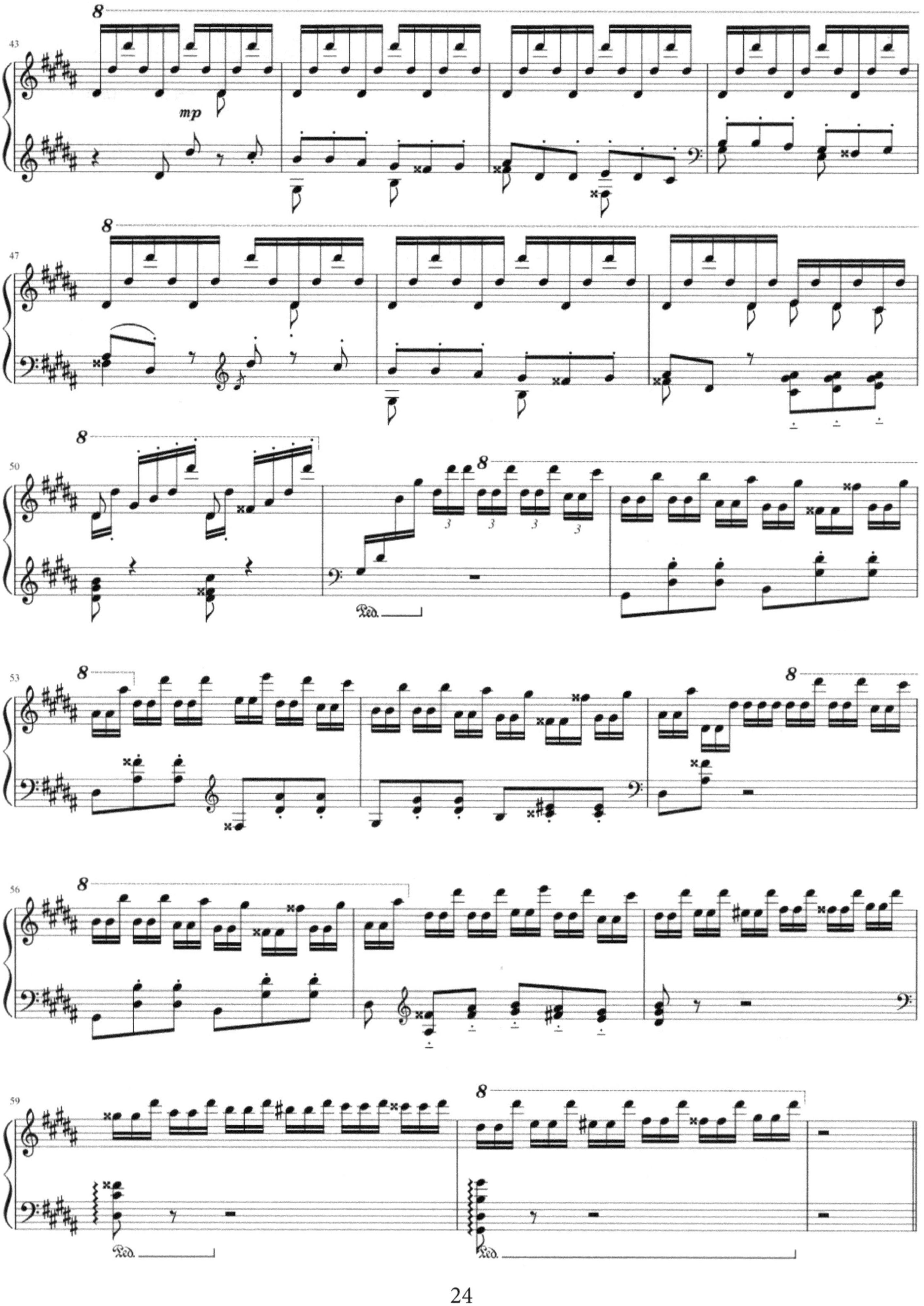

43
8
mp
47
8
50
8
8
3
3
3
3
Ped.
53
8
8
56
8
59
8
Ped.
Ped.

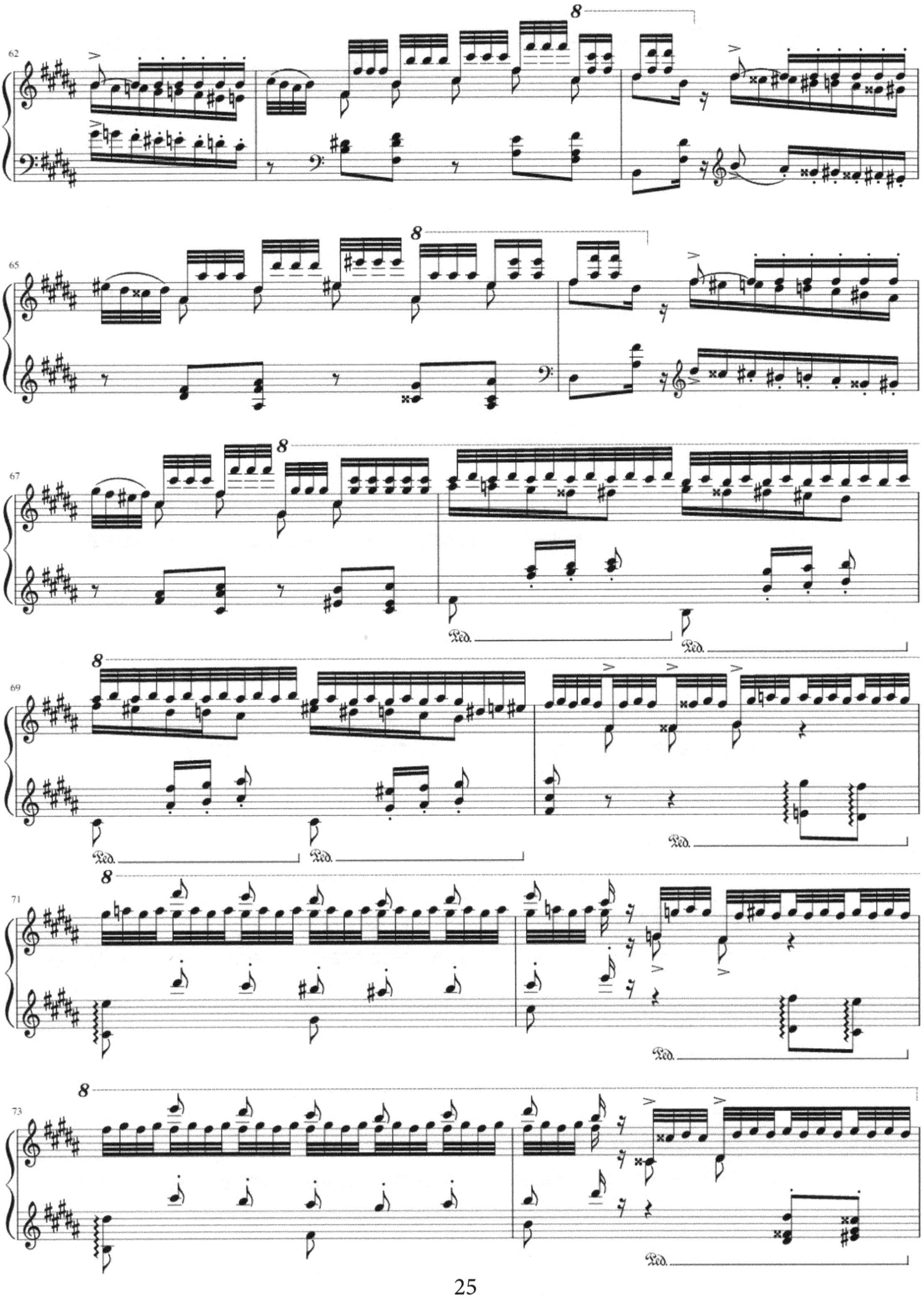
62
65
67
Ped.
69
71
73
8

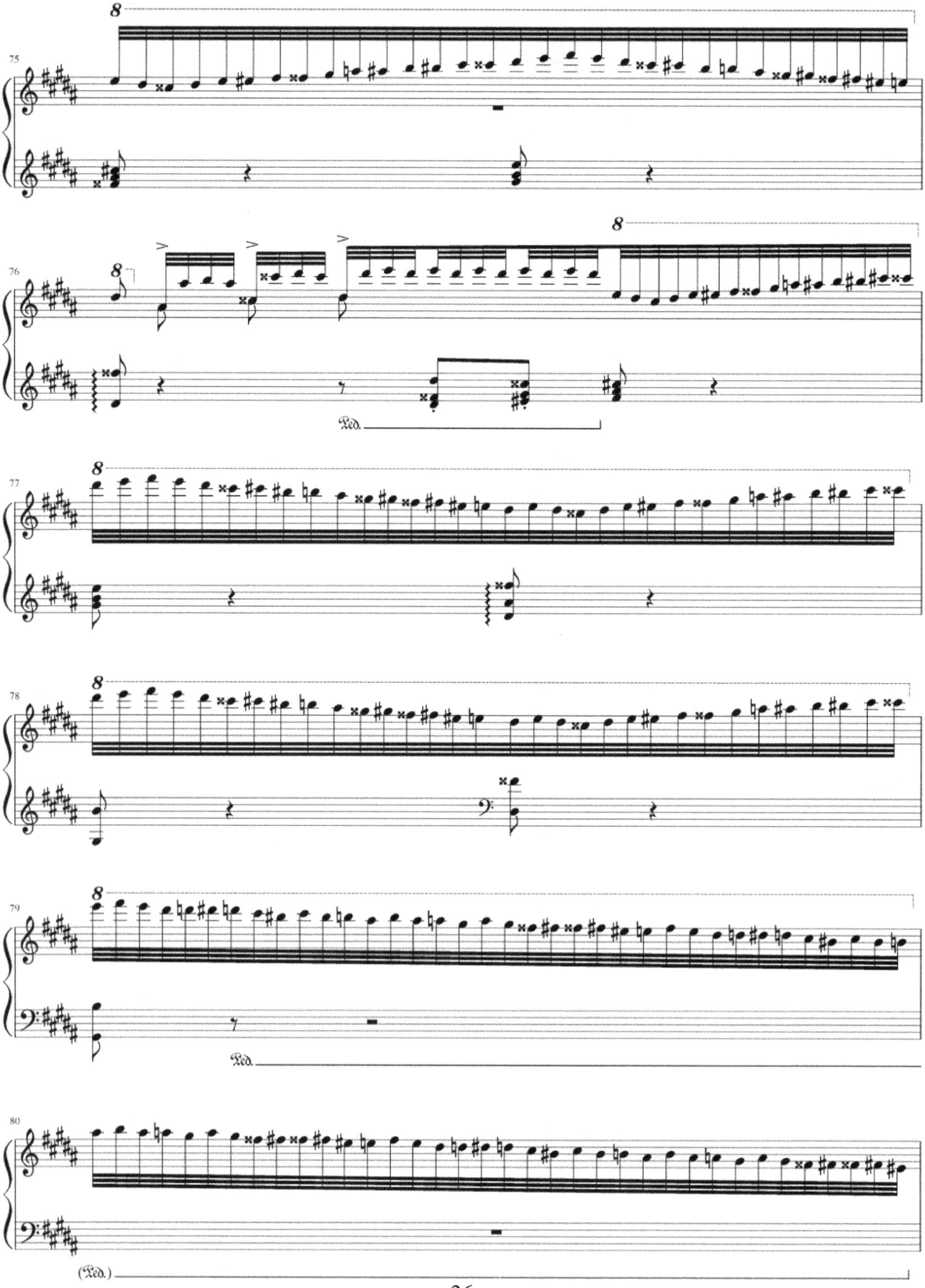
75
8
76
8
8
Ped.
77
8
78
8
79
8
Ped.
80
(Ped.)

81
𝄌𝄌Ped.
82
8
(Ped.)
83
8
f
ff
(Ped.)
85
8
p
Ped.
Ped.
Ped.
87
8
Ped.
Ped.
Ped.
89
8
mp
3

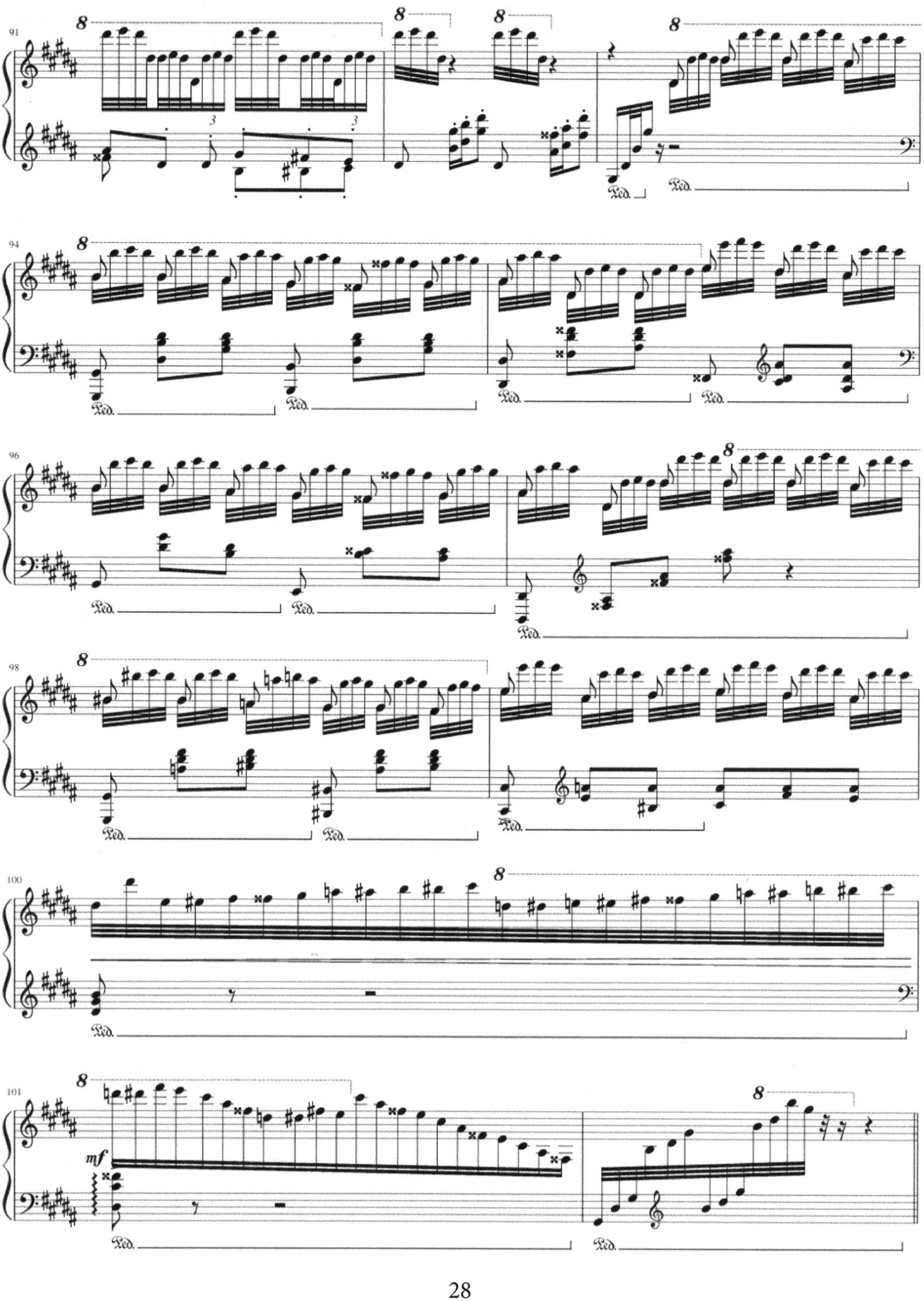
91
94
96
98
100
101
8
mf
Ped.

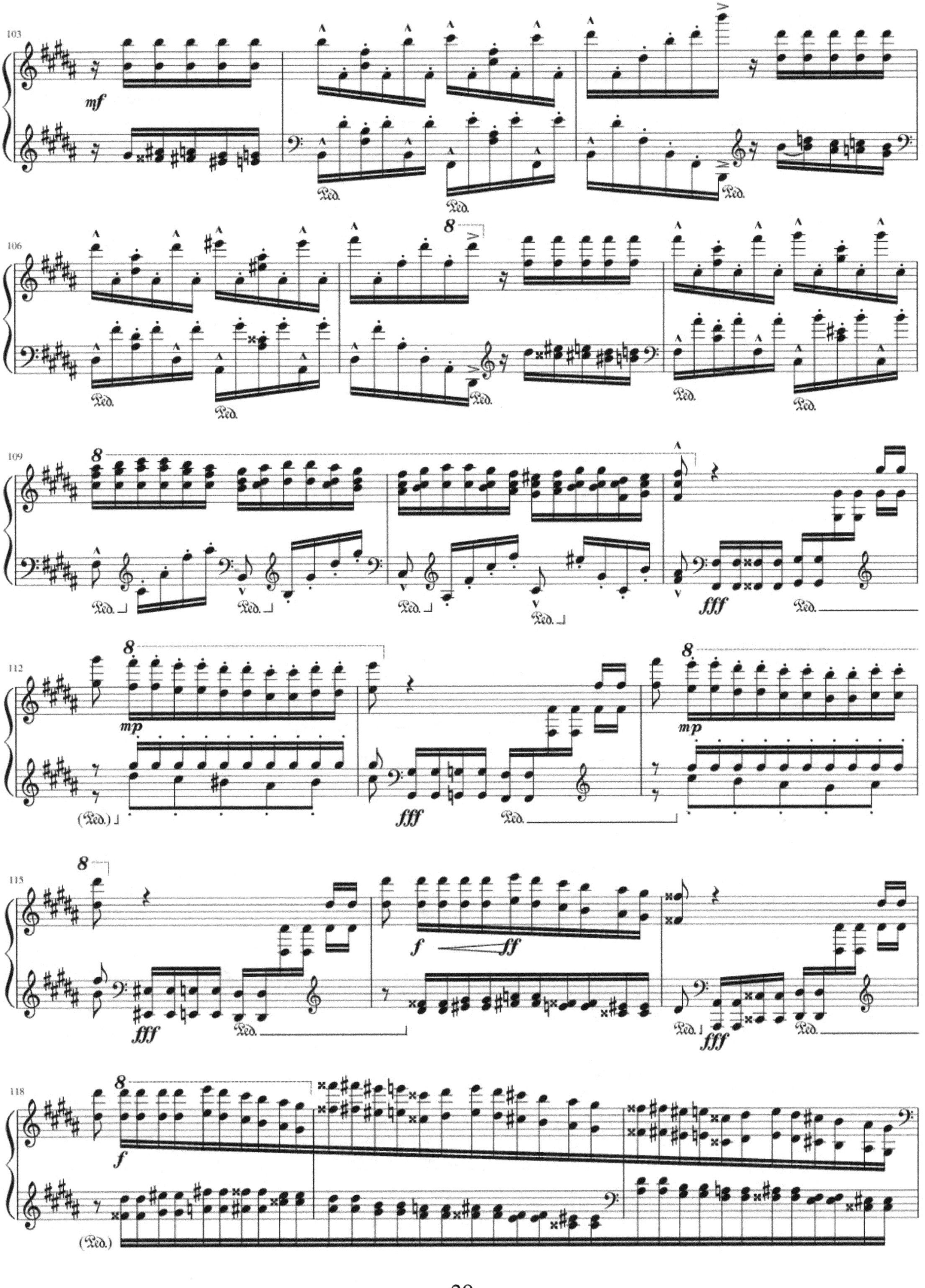

103
mf
106
109
fff
112
mp
fff
115
f
ff
118

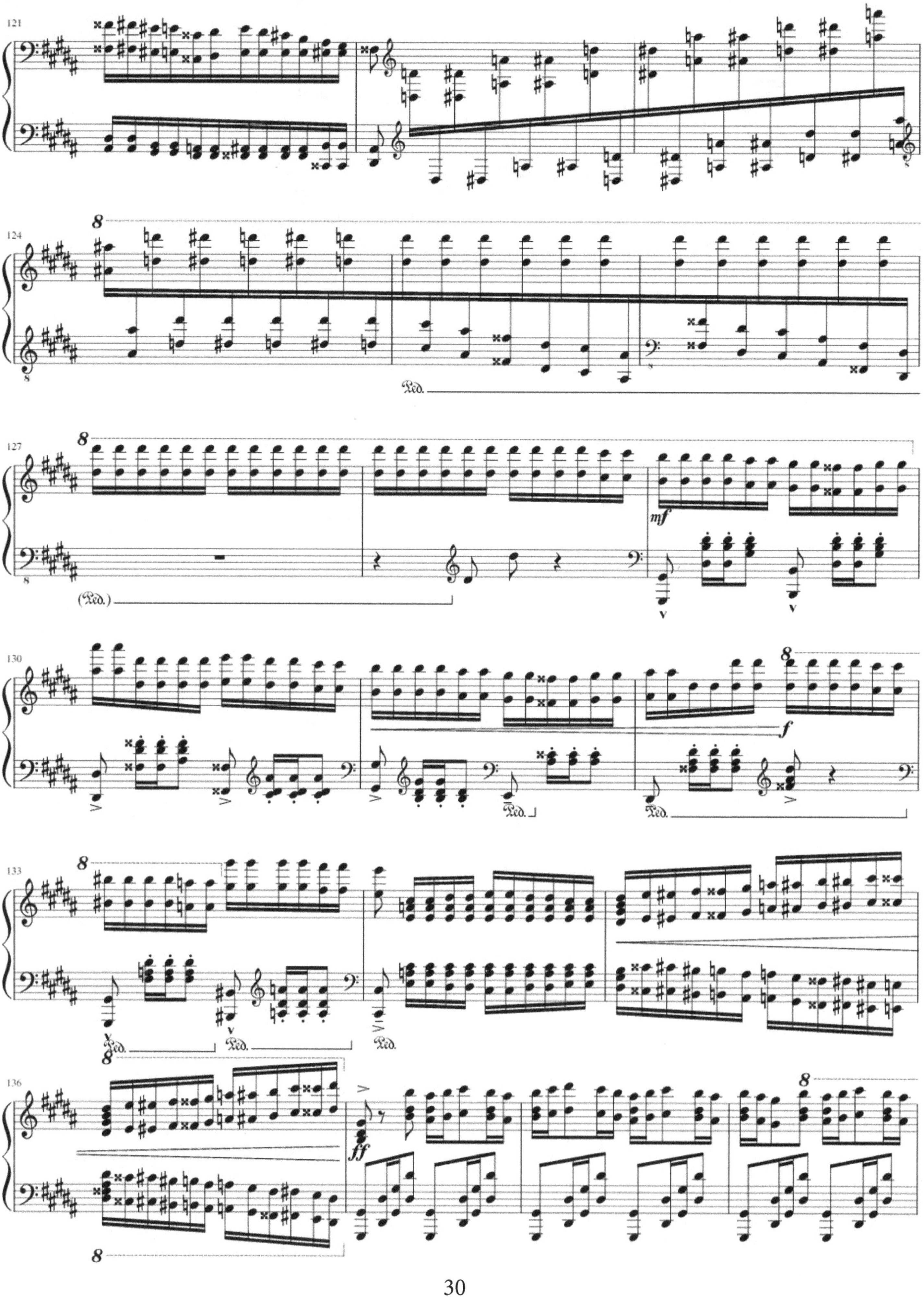
121
124
8
Ped.
127
8
(Ped.)
mf
130
8
f
Ped.
133
8
Ped.
Ped.
Ped.
136
8
ff
8

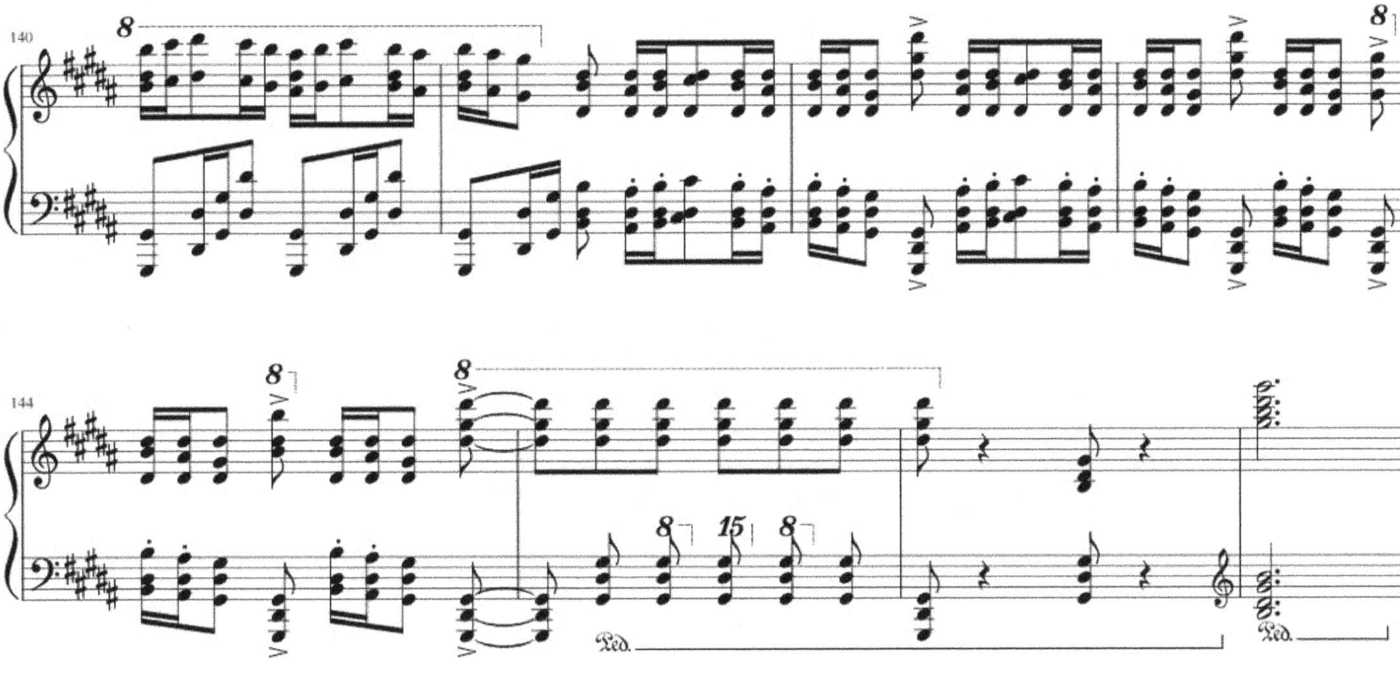
140
144
Ped.
Ped.

Wandered Fantasy in C Major

Opus 15

Allegro con fuoco ma non troppo.

Franz Schubert

33

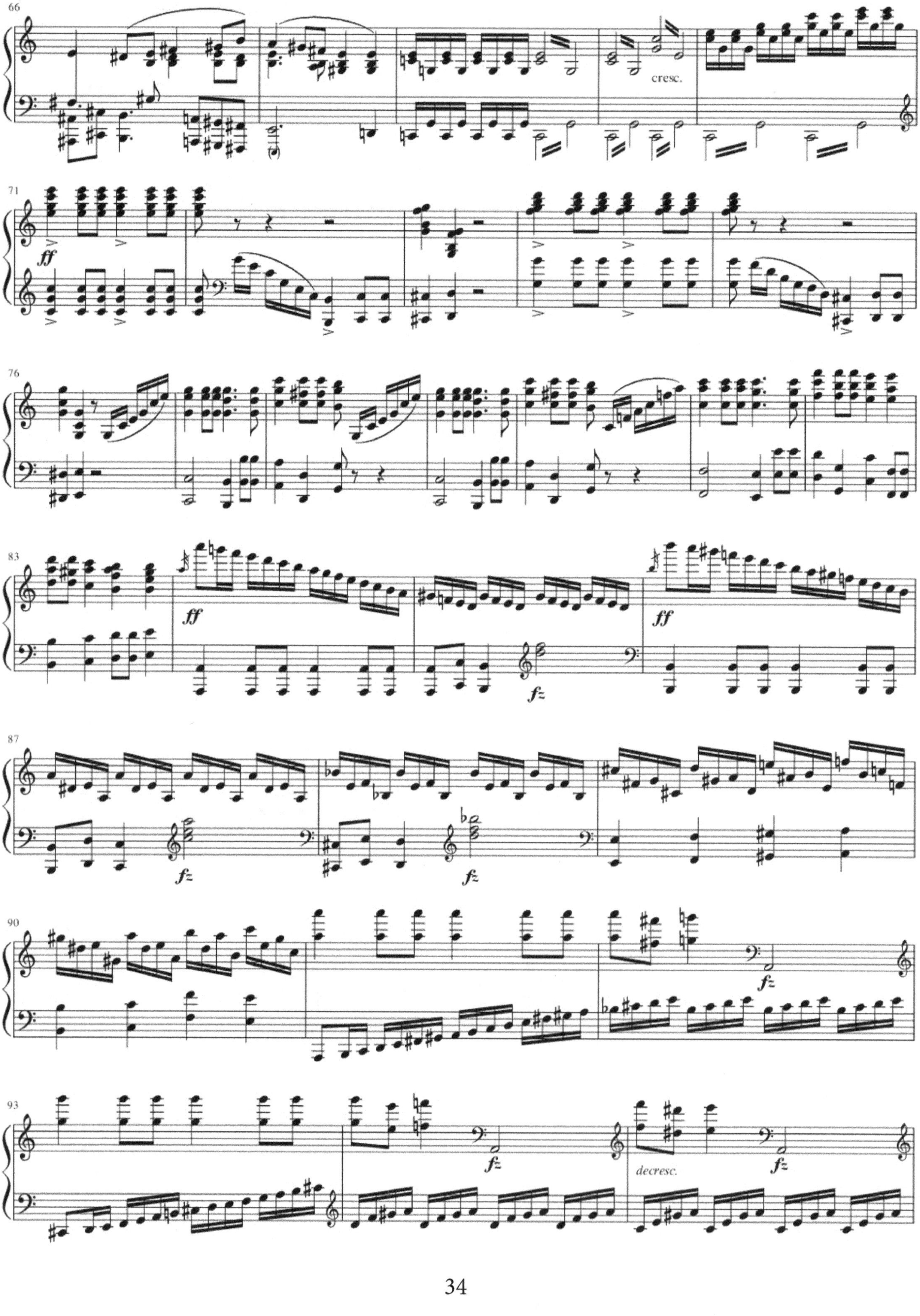
66
cresc.
71
ff
76
83
ff
ff
fz
87
fz
fz
90
fz
93
fz
decresc.
fz

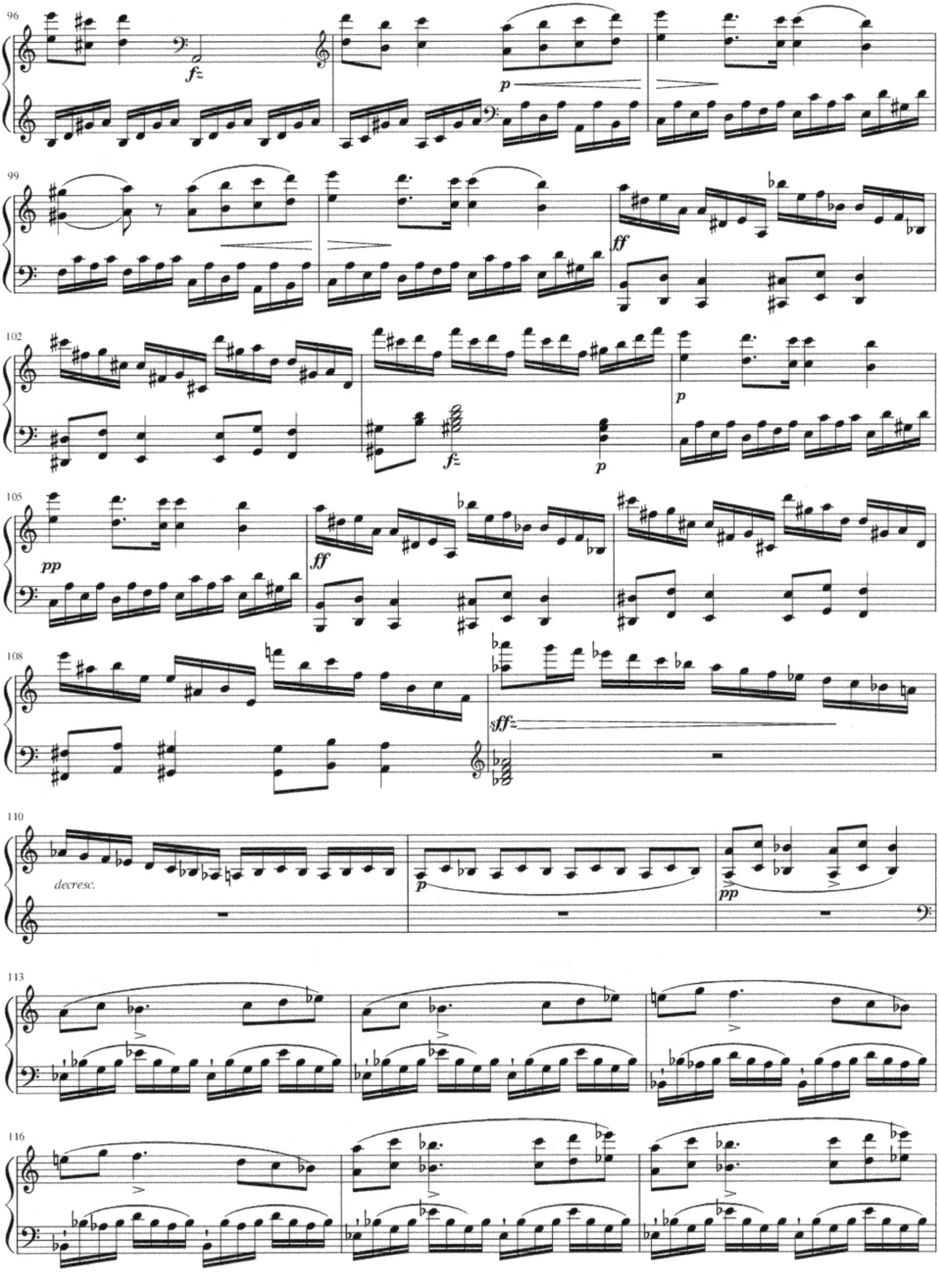
96
fz
p
99
ff
102
fz
p
p
105
pp
ff
108
sffz
110
decresc.
p
pp
113
116

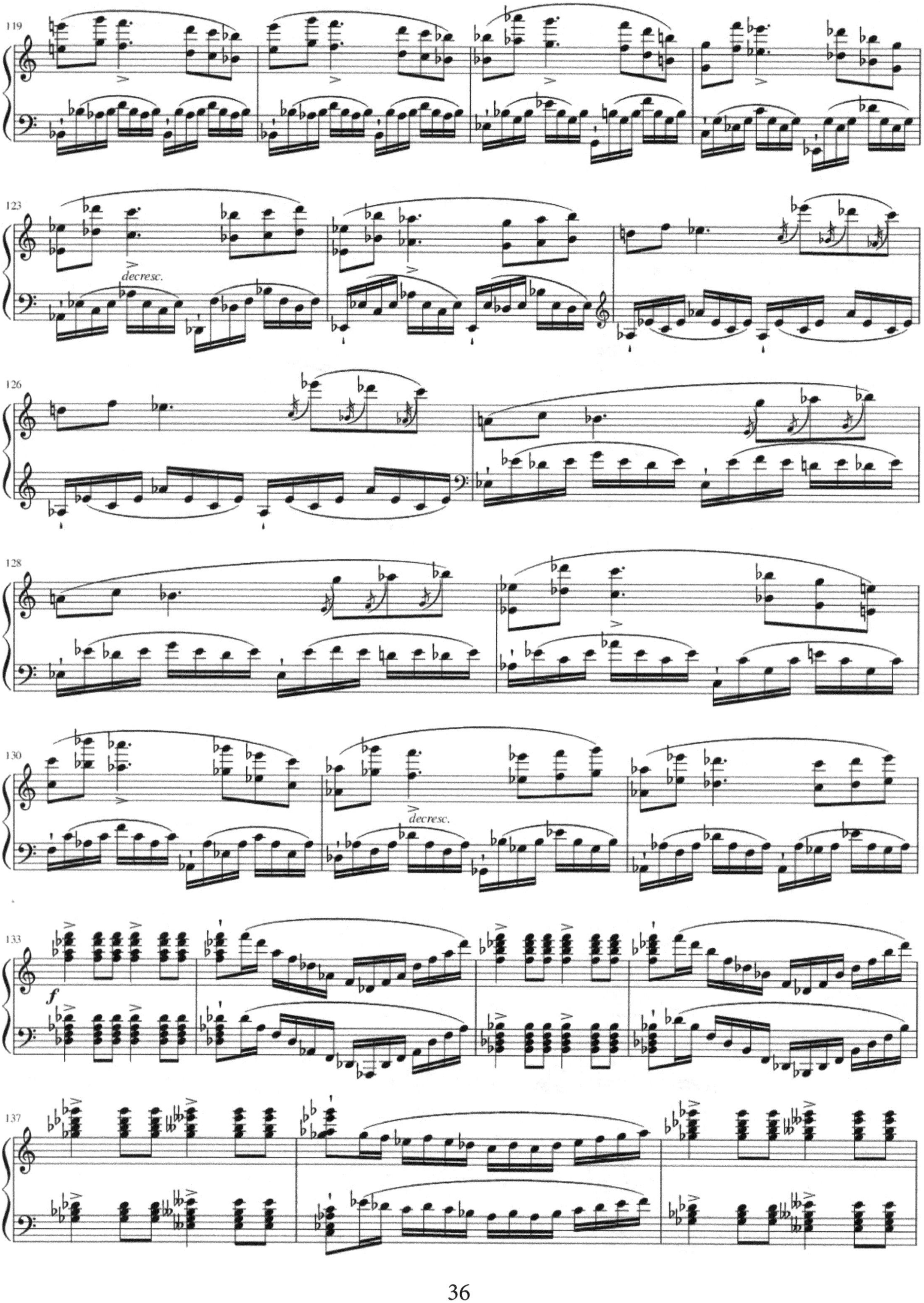
119
123
decresc.
126
128
130
decresc.
133
f
137

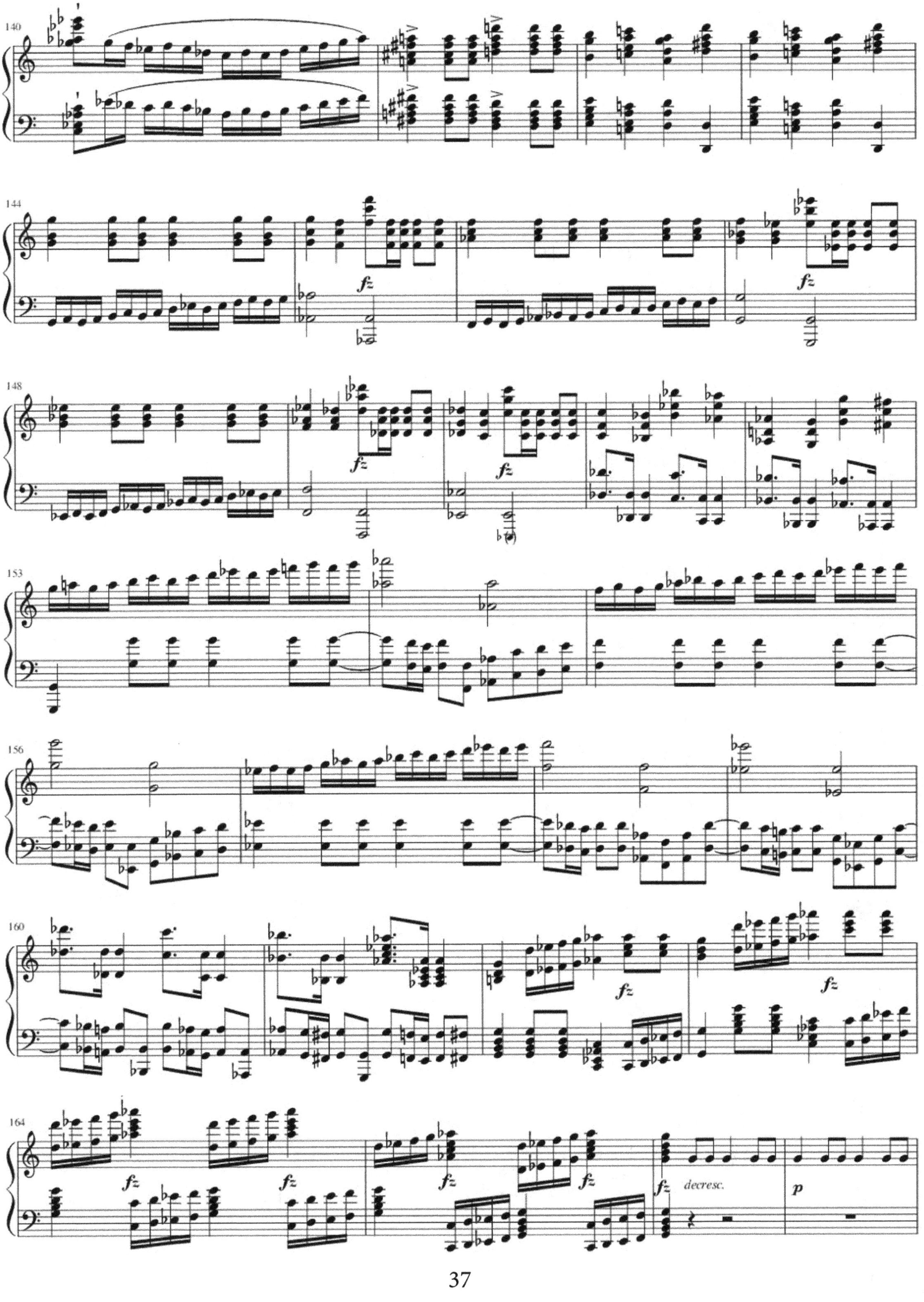
fz
decresc.
p

168
fz p
fz p
fz p
fz pp
fz pp
fz p fz p
175
fz p fz p
fz p fz p
fz pp fz pp
fz pp
179
ppp
183
189
Adagio
pp
5
195
pp
5
pp
199
dim.

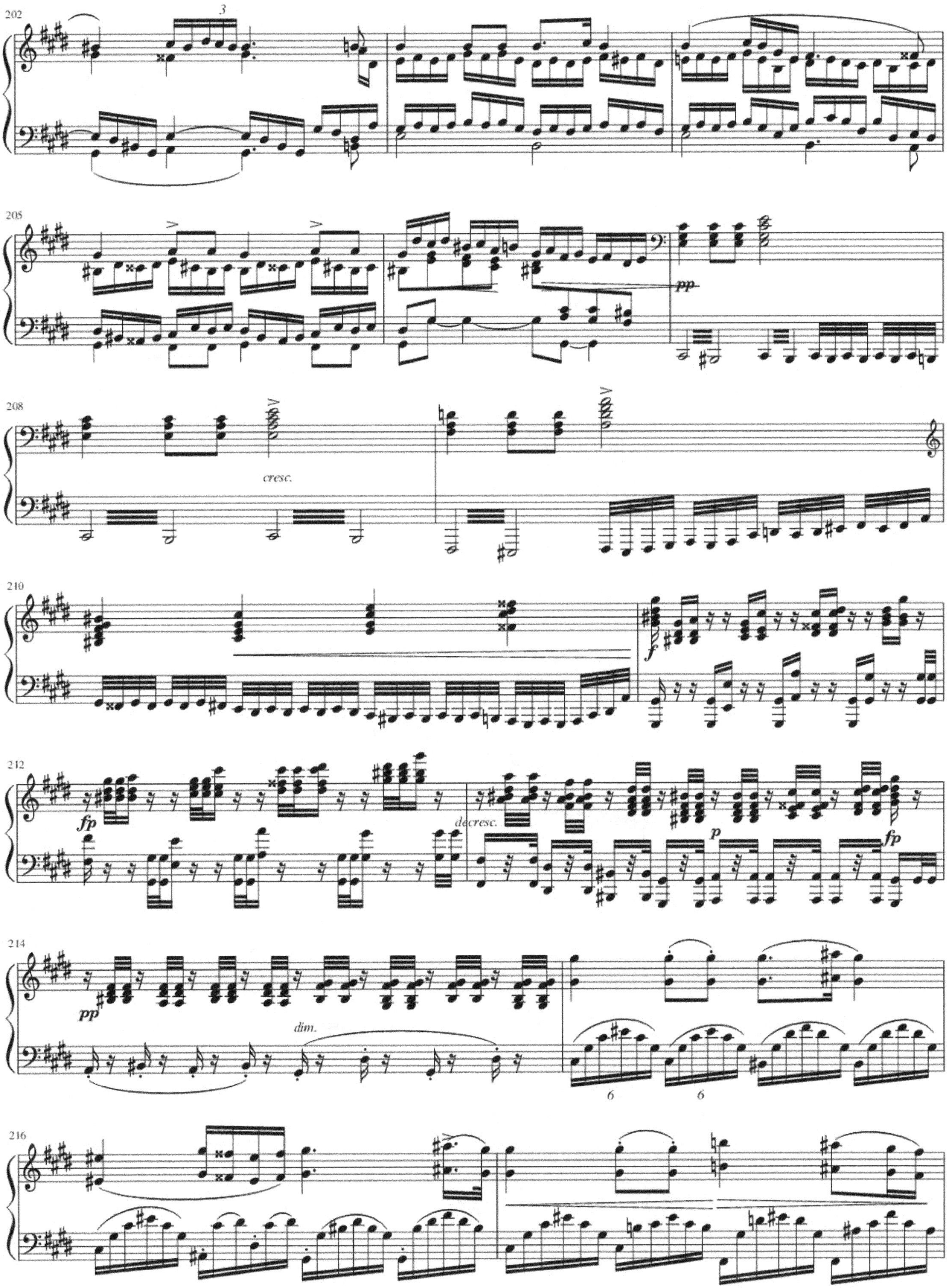
202
205
pp
208
cresc.
210
f
212
fp
decresc.
p
fp
214
pp
dim.
216

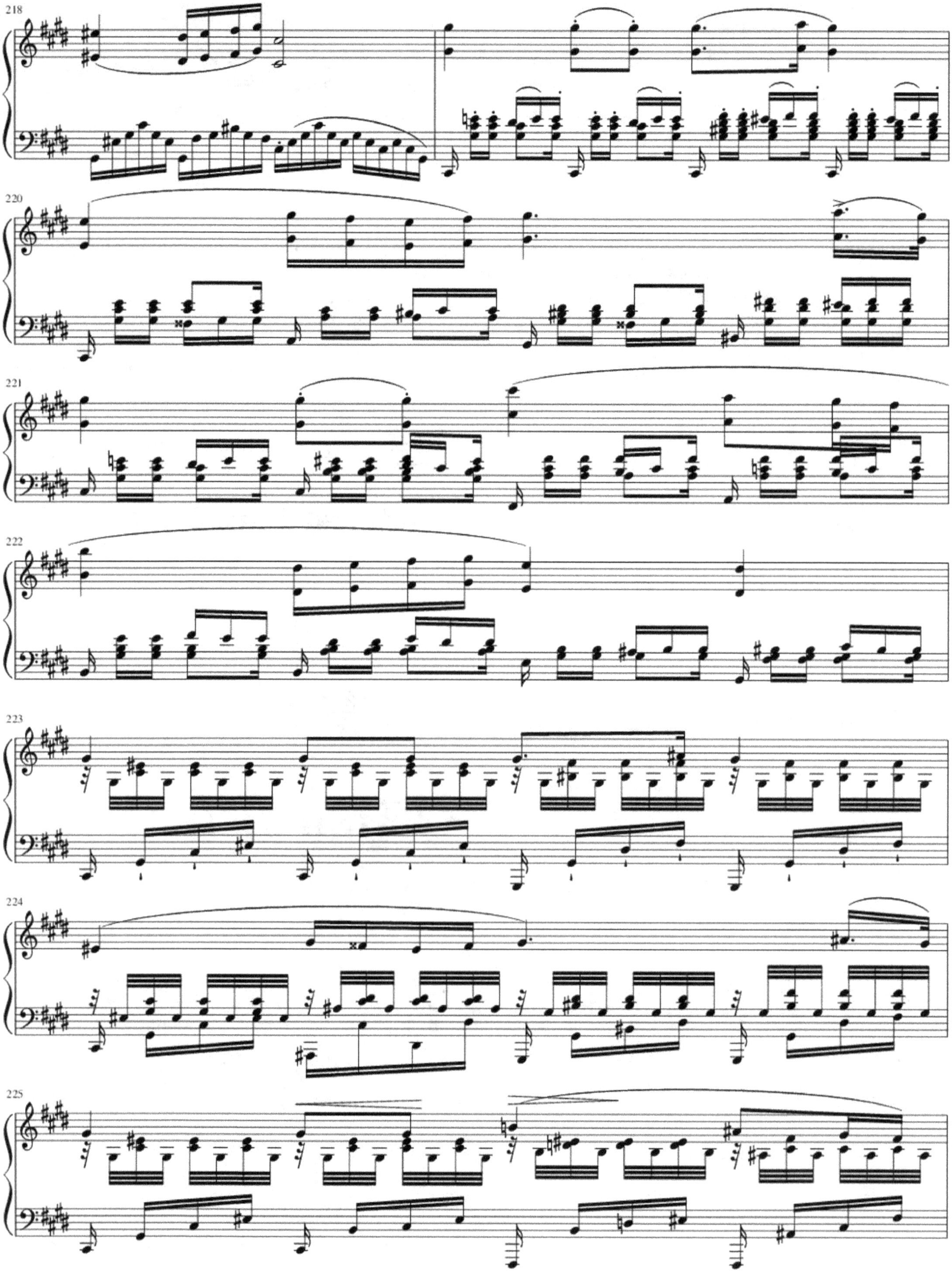
218
220
221
222
223
224
225

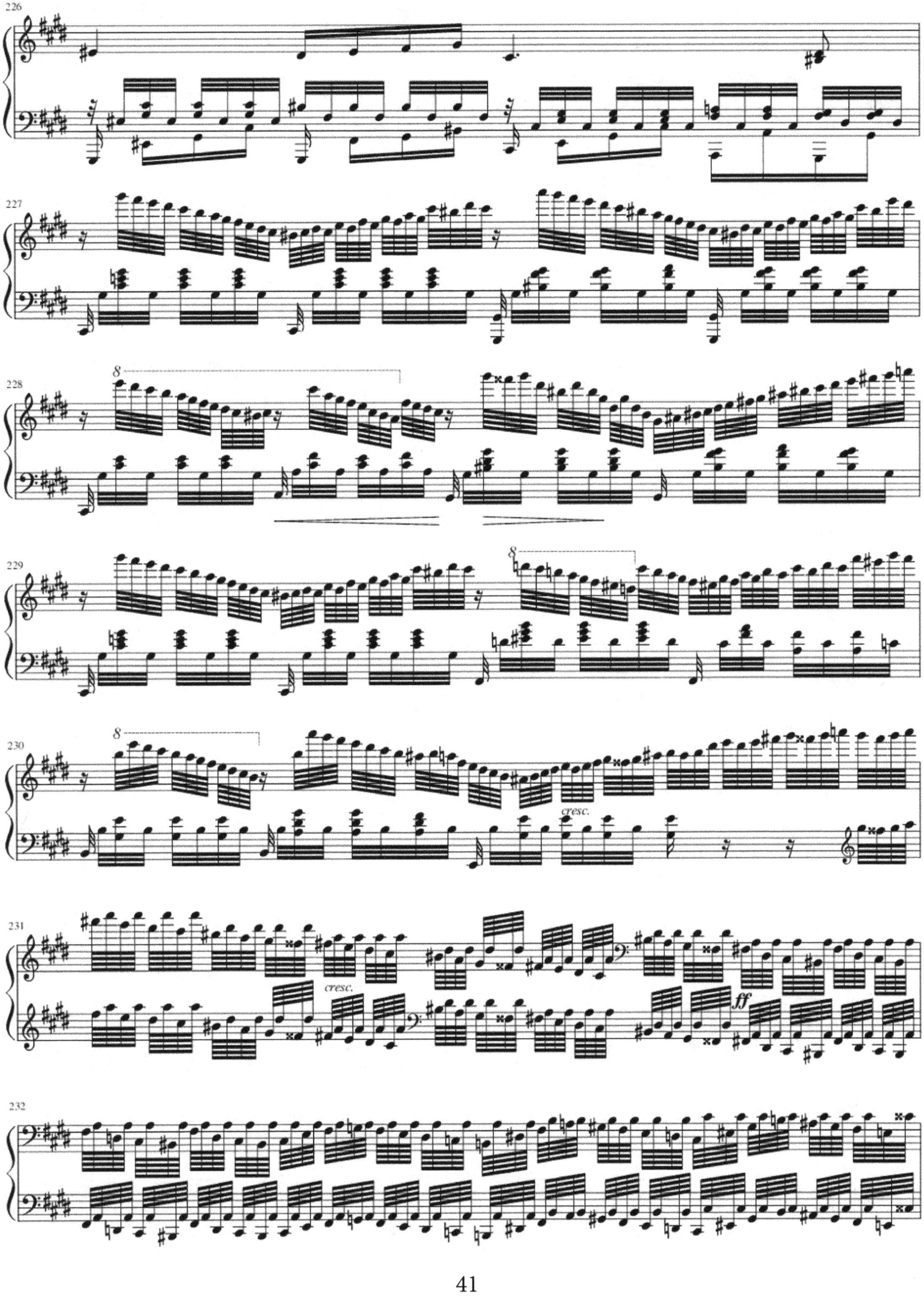
226
227
228
8
229
8
230
8
cresc.
231
cresc.
ff
232

233
234
ff
235
fz
fz
fz
fz
236
fp
tremolo
pp
dim.
237
238
239
tremelo
pp

43

270
ff
pp
279
fz
288
cresc.
f
297
cresc.
ff
fz
ff
fz
305
fz
fz
fz
fz
311
fz
fz
fz
fz
cresc.
fz
fz
fz
319
ff
fz
fp
p

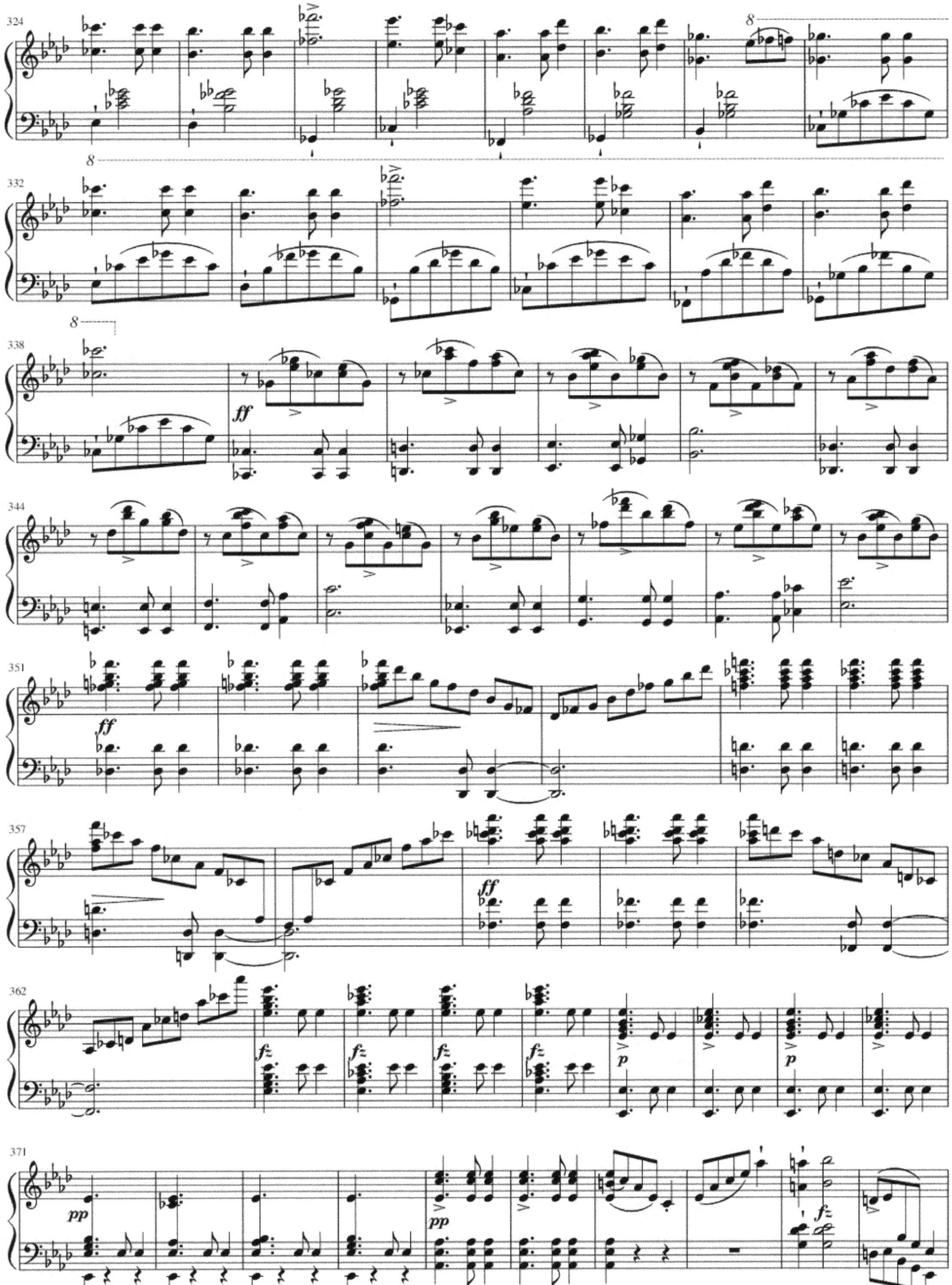
324
8
332
338
ff
344
351
ff
357
ff
362
fz
p
371
pp

381
fz
ff
389
fz
p
f
ff
397
cresc.
ff
fz
p
pp
406
8
416
8
ff
pp
427
pp
439
450

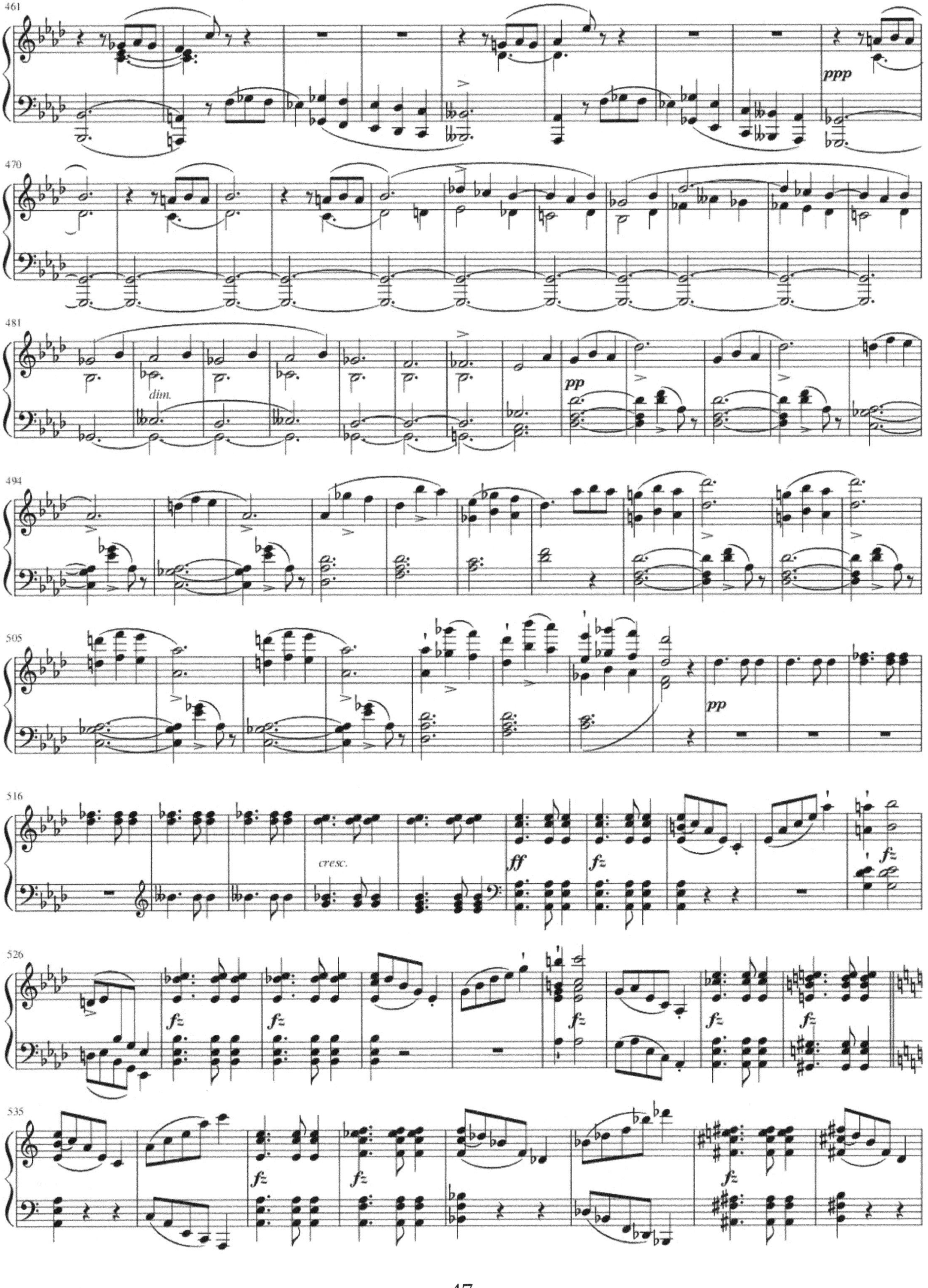
461
ppp
470
481
dim.
pp
494
505
pp
516
cresc.
ff
fz
526
fz
535
fz

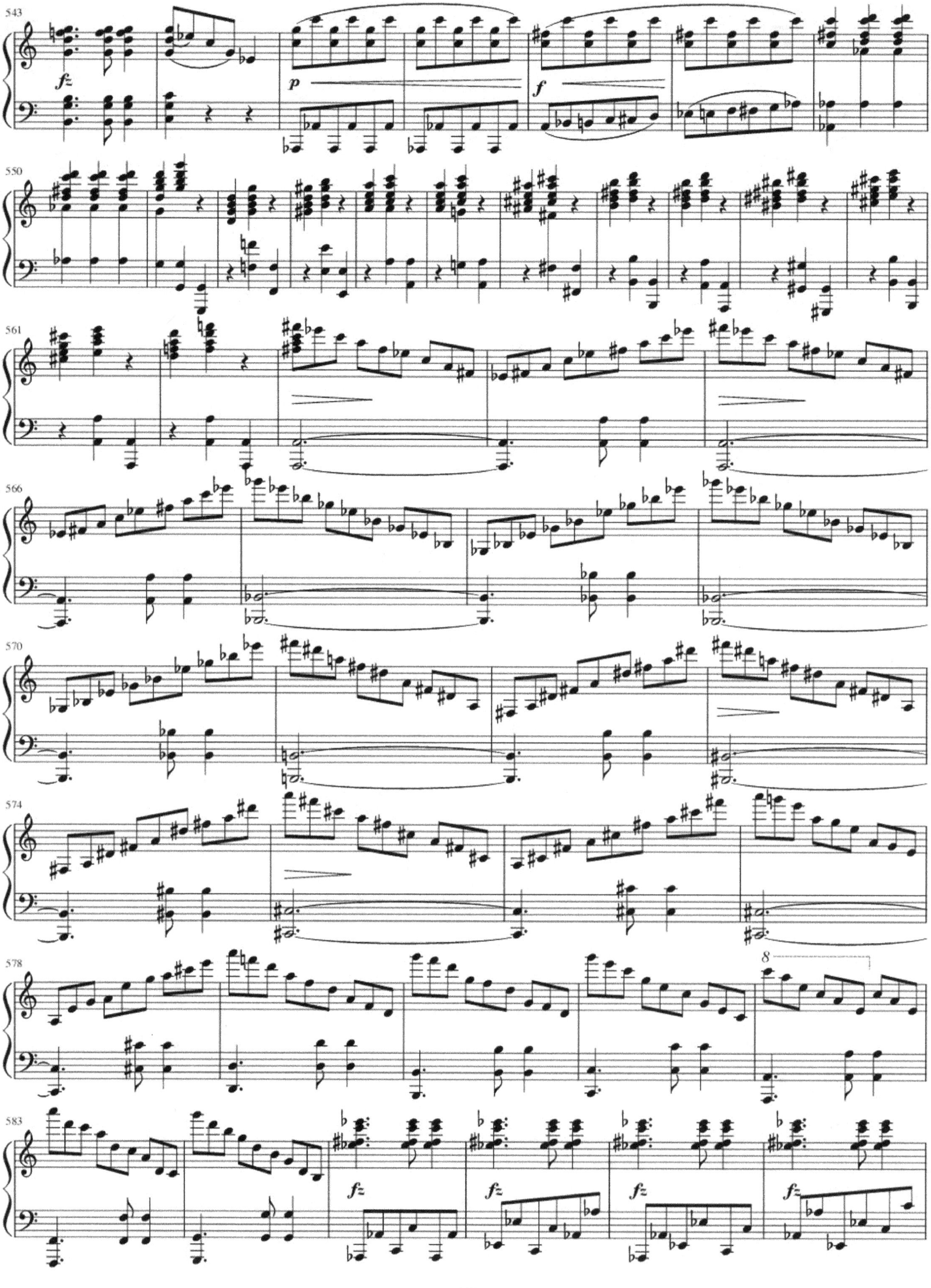
543
fz
p
f
550
561
566
570
574
578
8
583
fz
fz
fz
fz

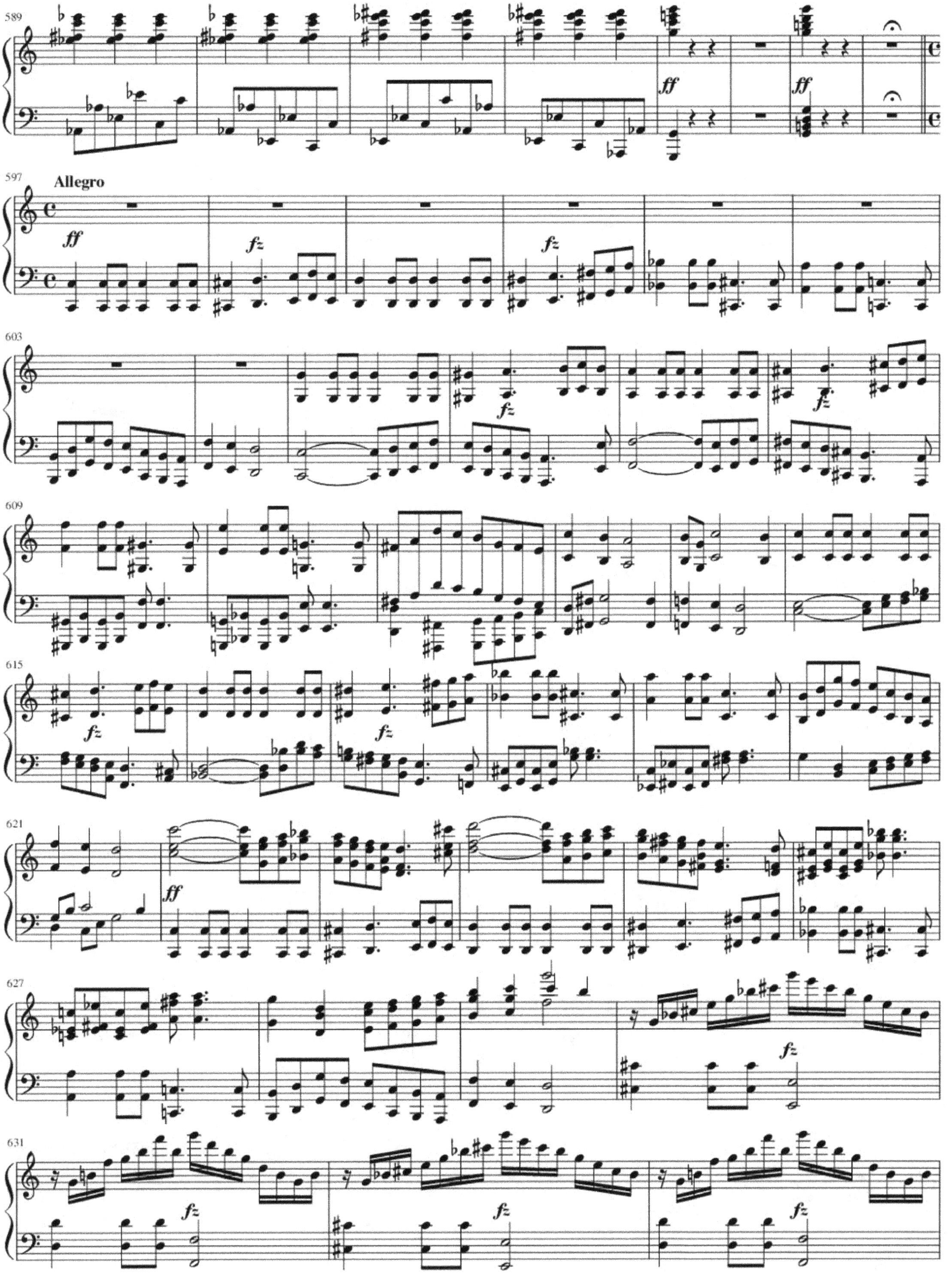
Allegro
ff
fz

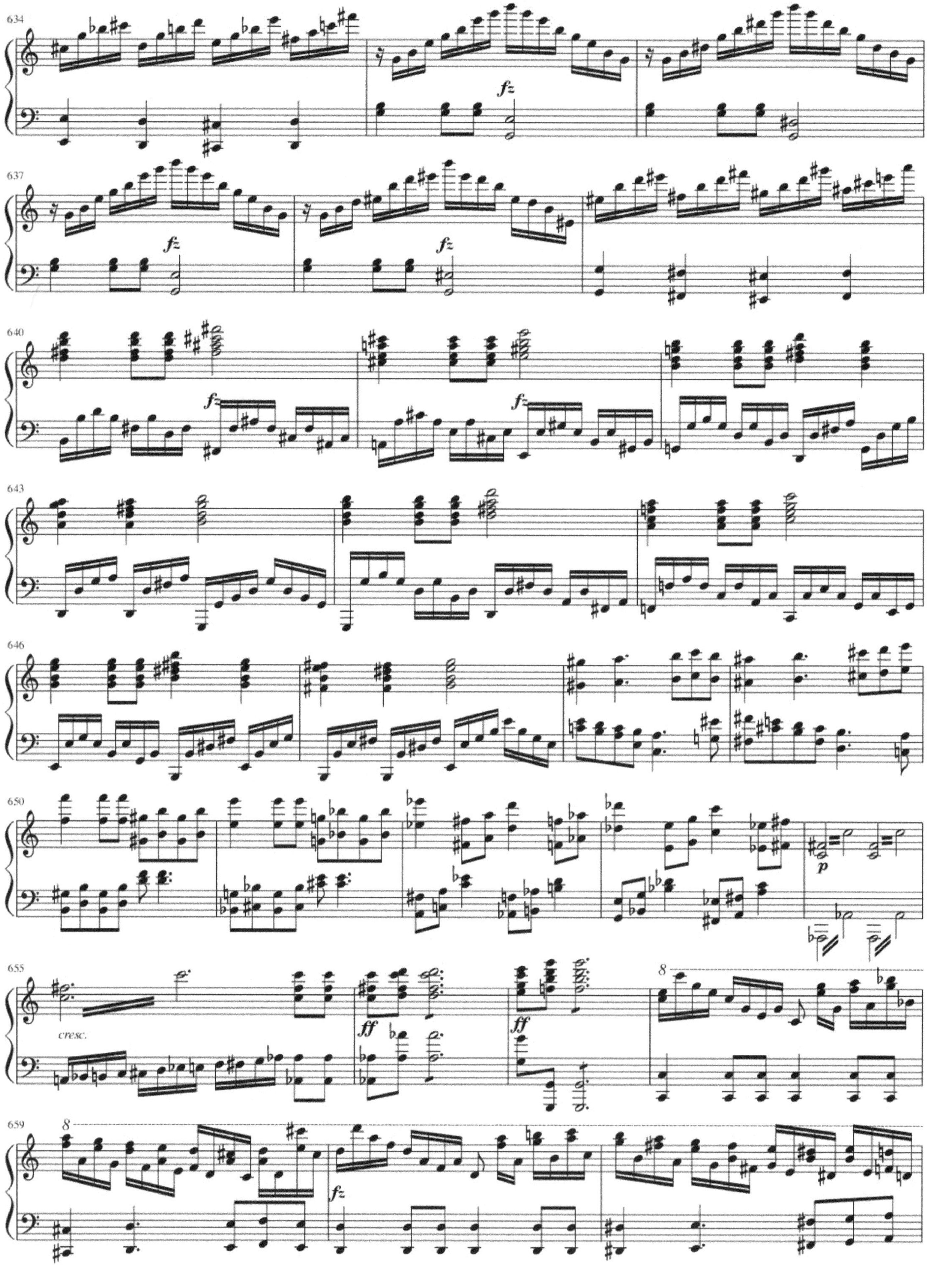
634
fz
637
fz
fz
640
fz
fz
643
646
650
p
655
cresc.
ff
ff
8
659
8
fz

662
8
665
p
cresc.
669
ff
p
cresc.
ff
674
p
678
cresc.
681
f
ff
684
687

690
fz
693
p
696
cresc.
699
cresc.
703
p
cresc.
706
f
cresc.
709
ff
fff
712

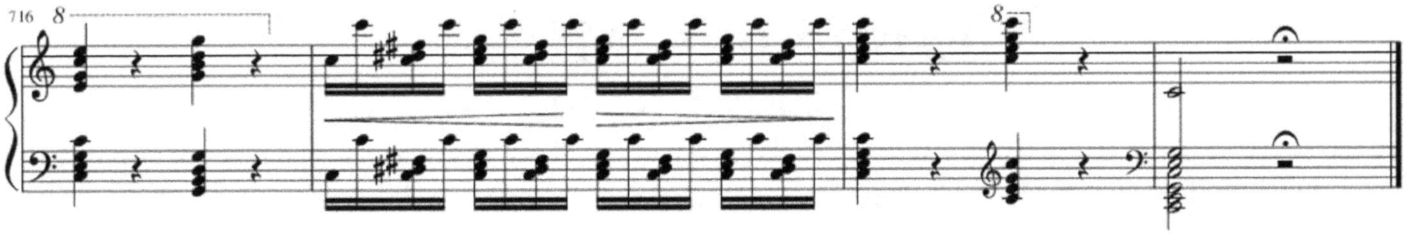
716
8
8

Etude in C Minor

Opus 25, No 12

Frédéric François Chopin

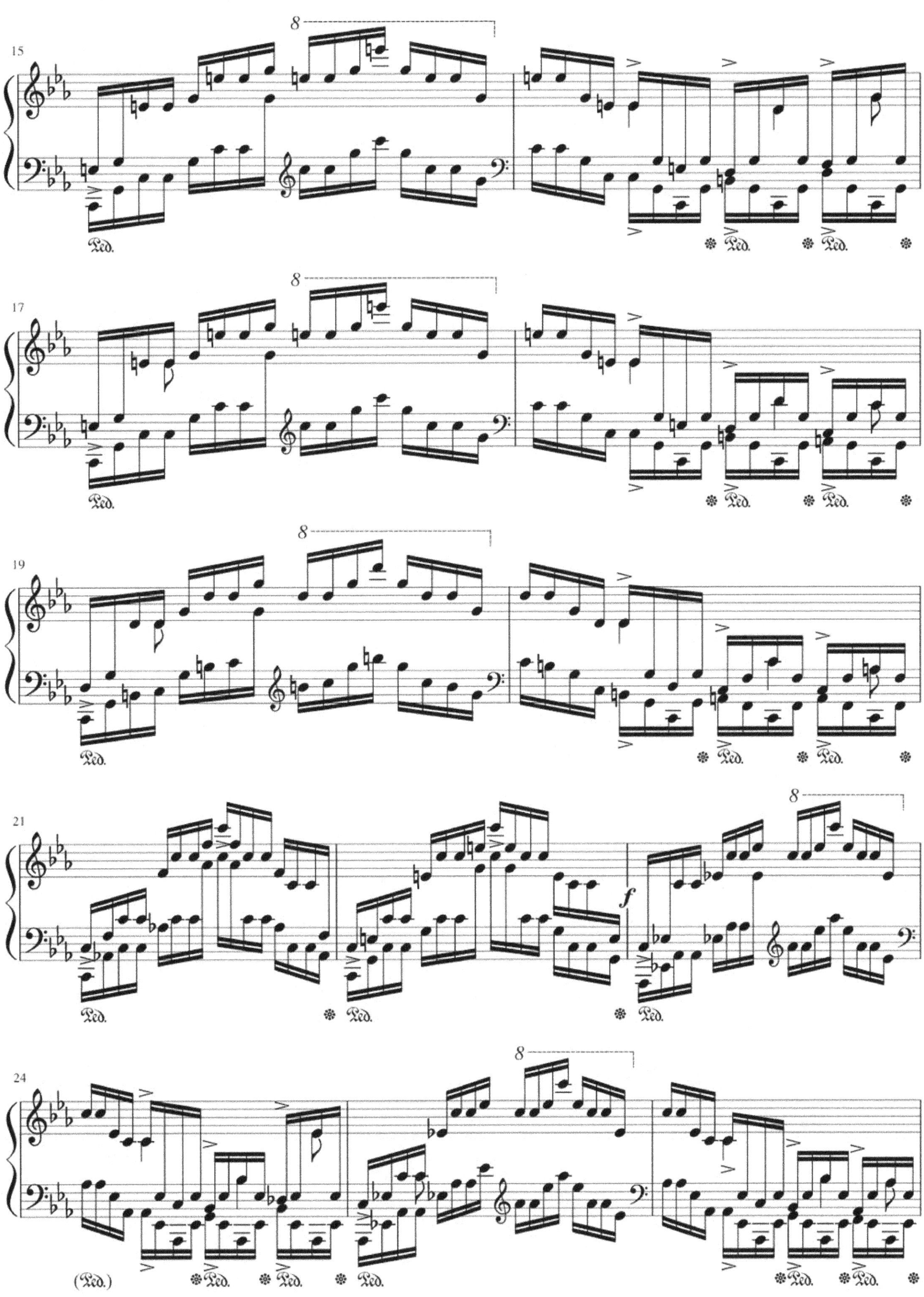

15
8
Ped.
17
19
21
f
24
(Ped.)

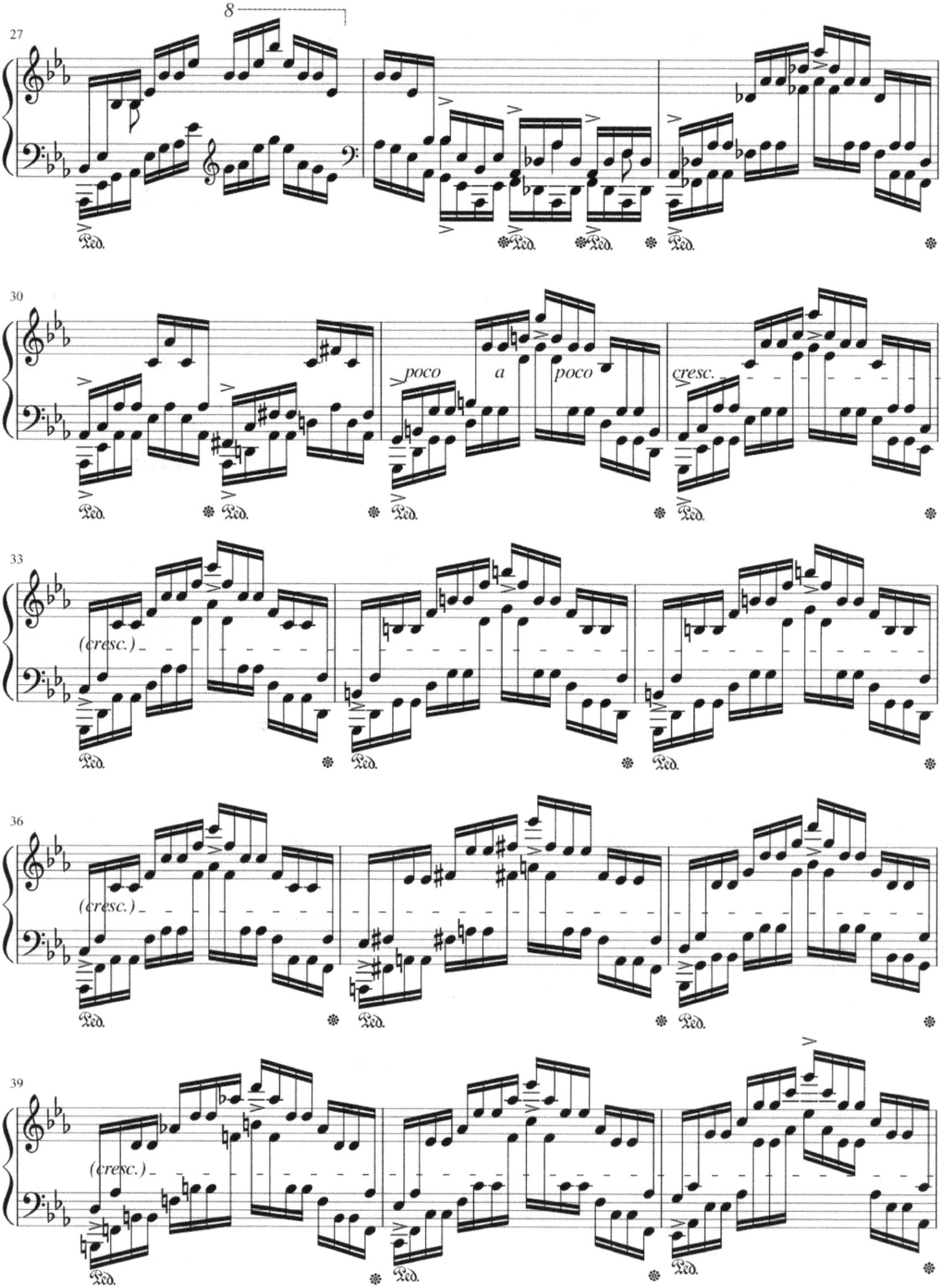
27
8
Ped.
30
poco
a
poco
cresc.
33
(cresc.)
36
(cresc.)
39
(cresc.)

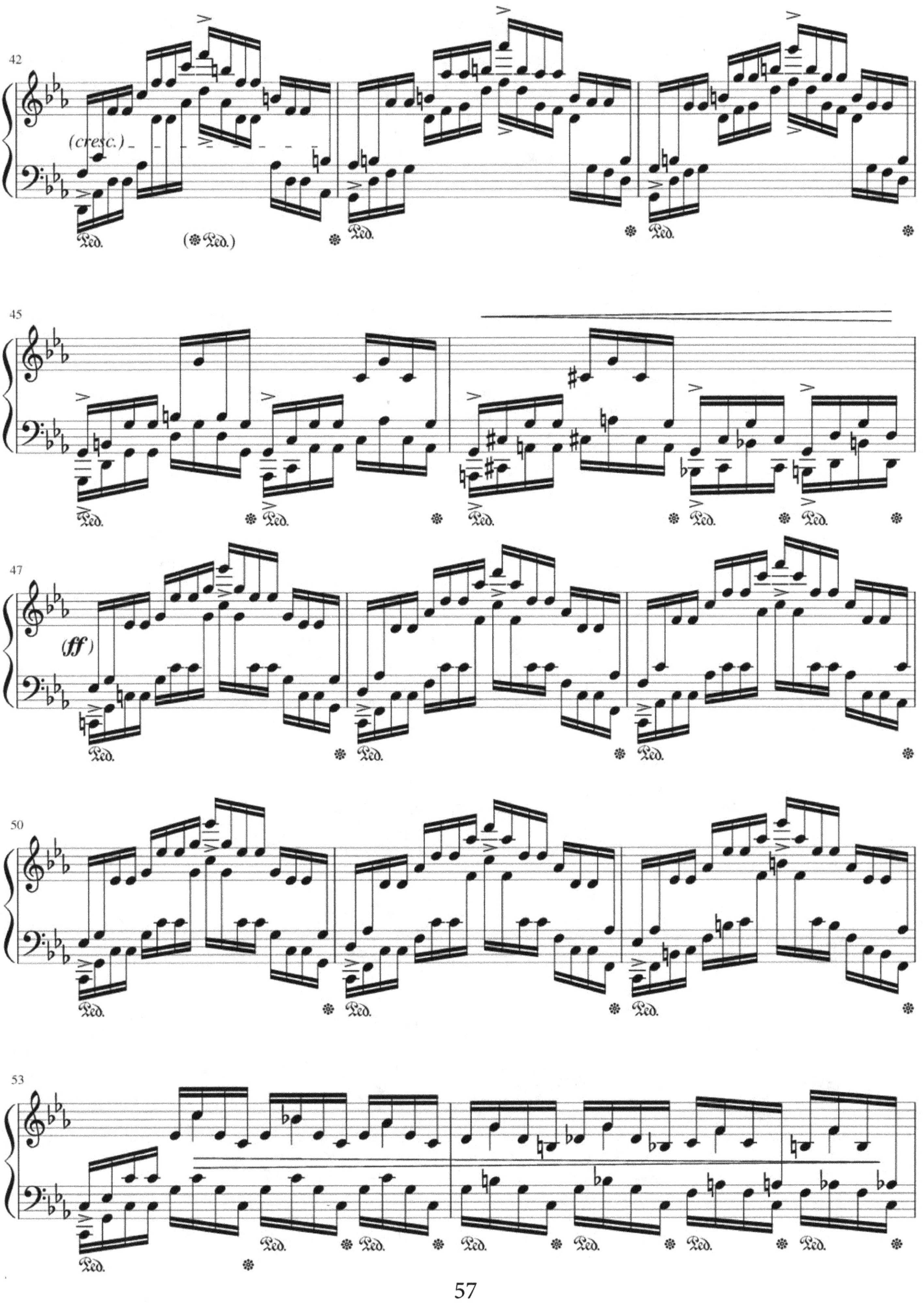
42
(cresc.)
Ped.
(✻Ped.)
45
Ped.
47
(ff)
Ped.
50
Ped.
53
Ped.

55
cresc.
58
(cresc.)
61
(cresc.)
64
8
(cresc.)
67
il più forte possibile
Ped.

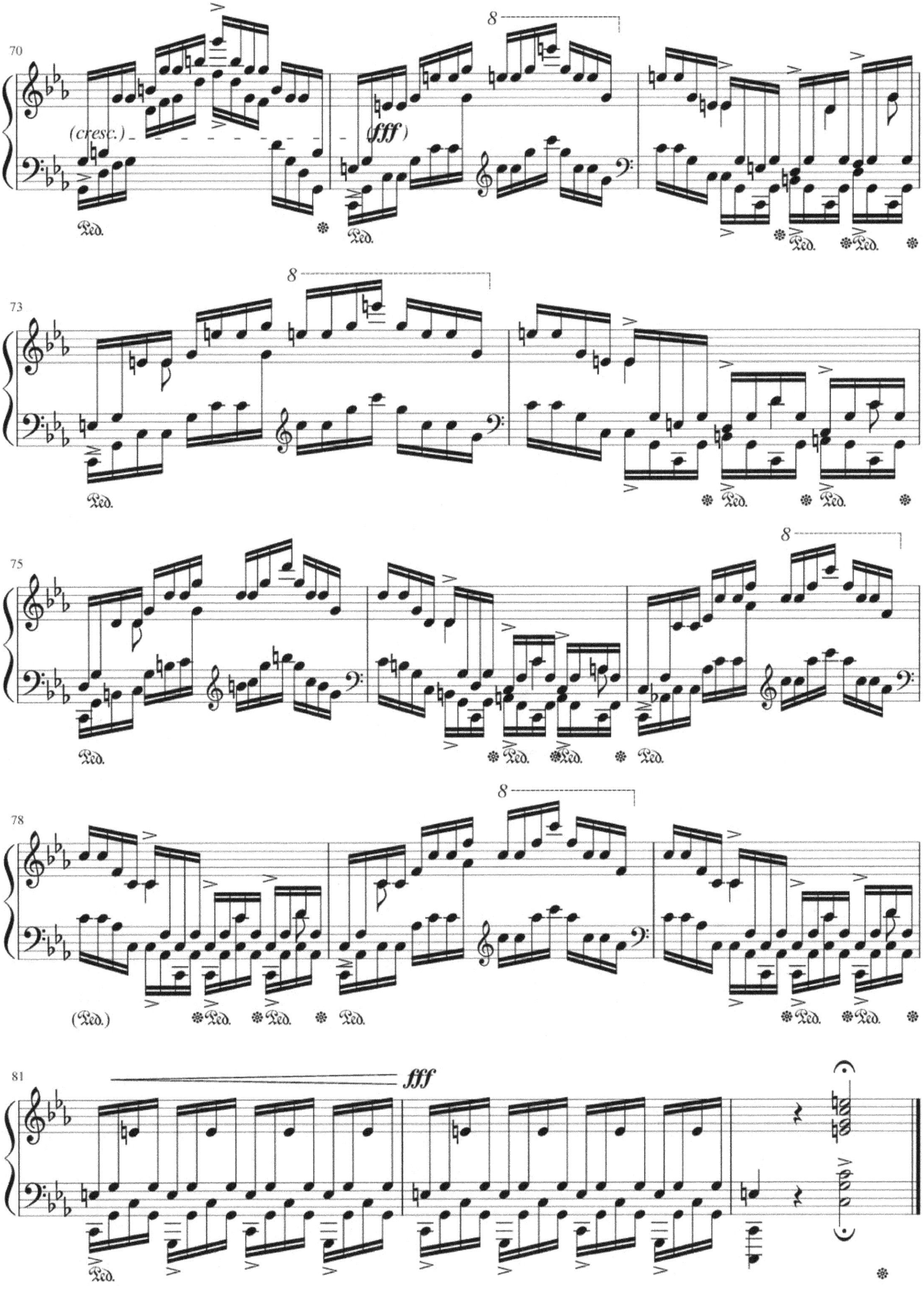

(cresc.)
(fff)
Ped.
(Ped.)
fff

Fantaisie Impromptu
Opus 66

Frédéric François Chopin

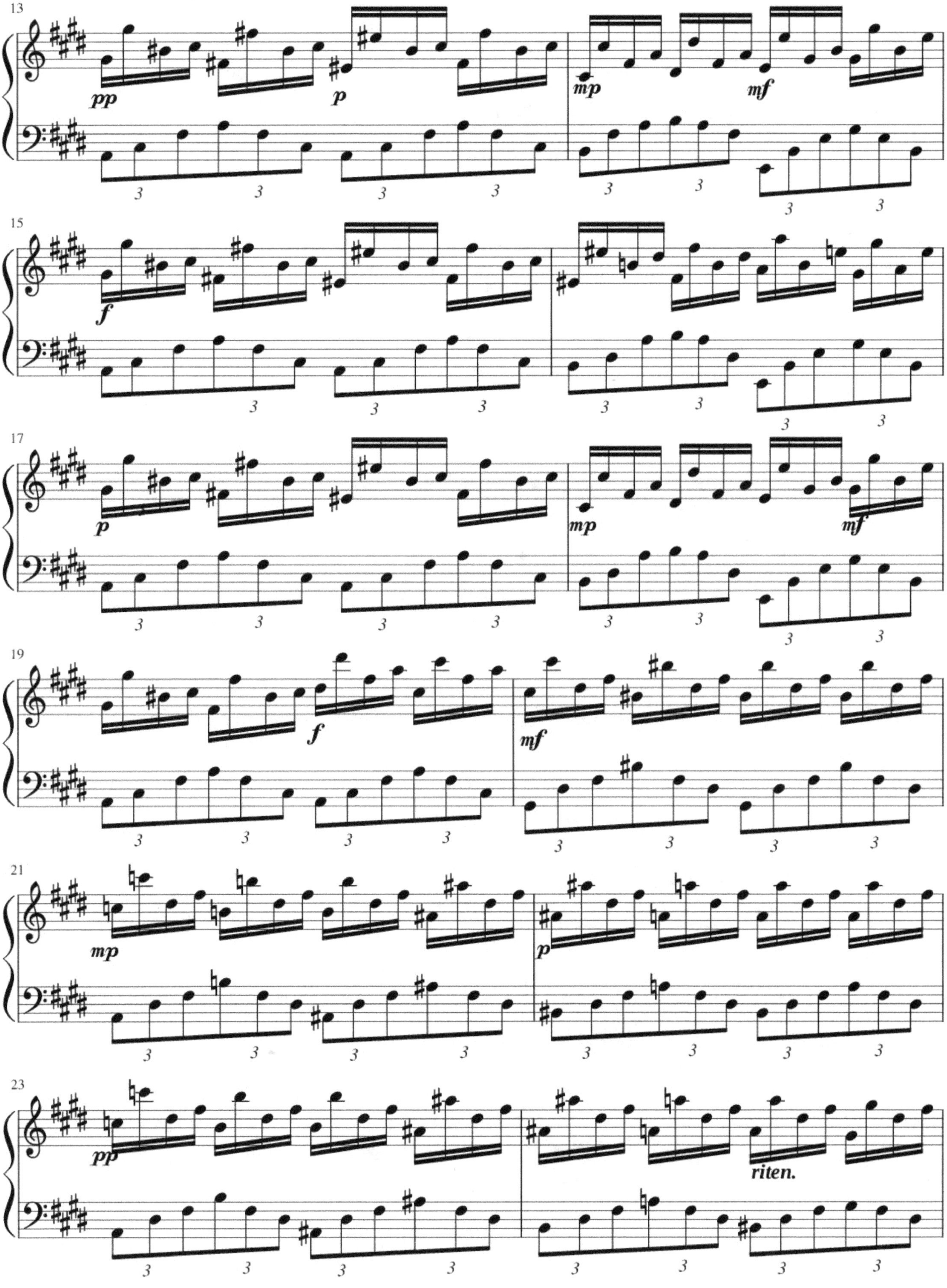
13
pp
p
mp
mf
15
f
17
p
mp
mf
19
f
mf
21
mp
p
23
pp
riten.

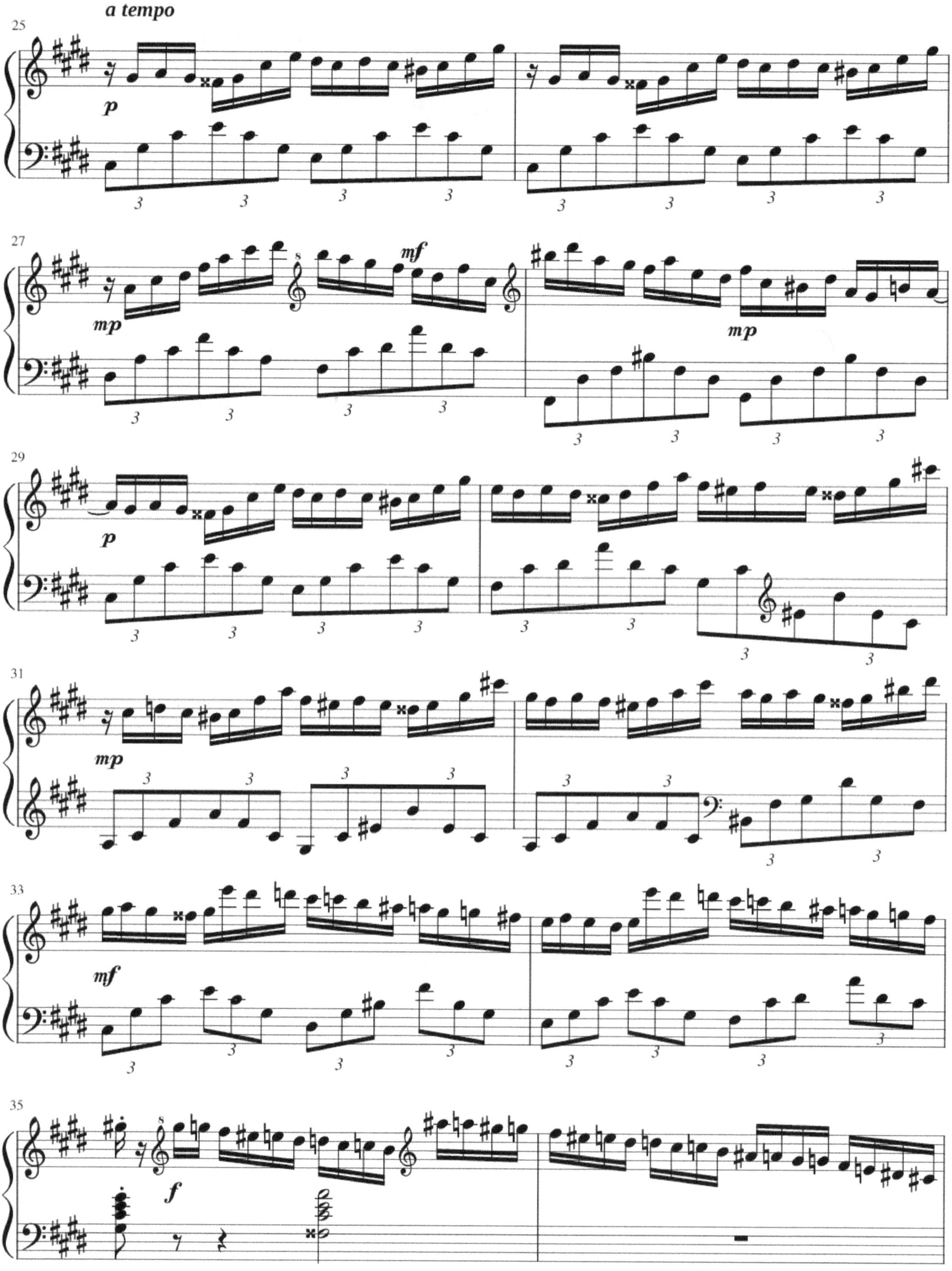
a tempo
25
p
27
mp
mf
mp
29
p
31
mp
33
mf
35
f

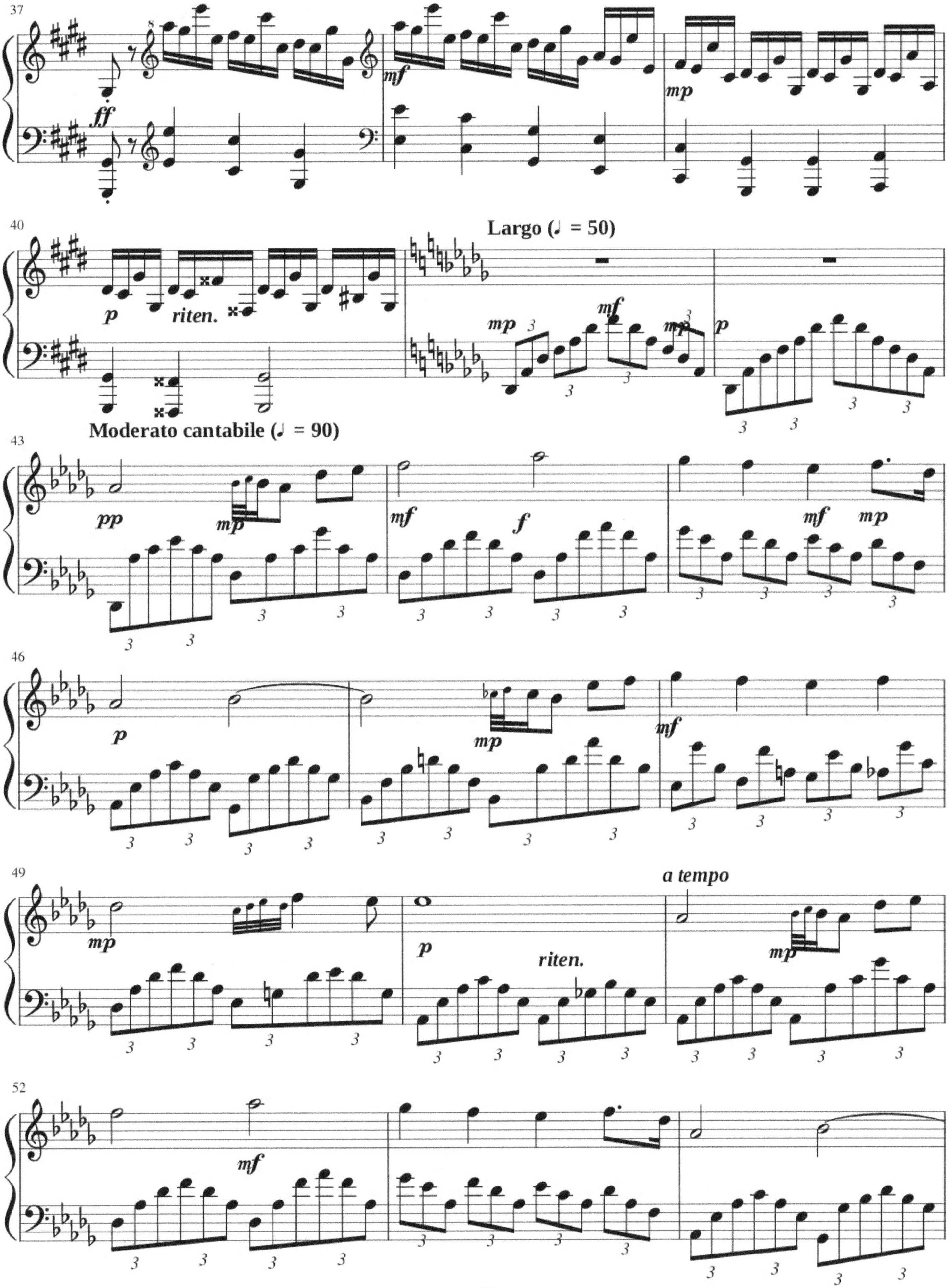

riten.
Largo (♩ = 50)
Moderato cantabile (♩ = 90)
riten.
a tempo

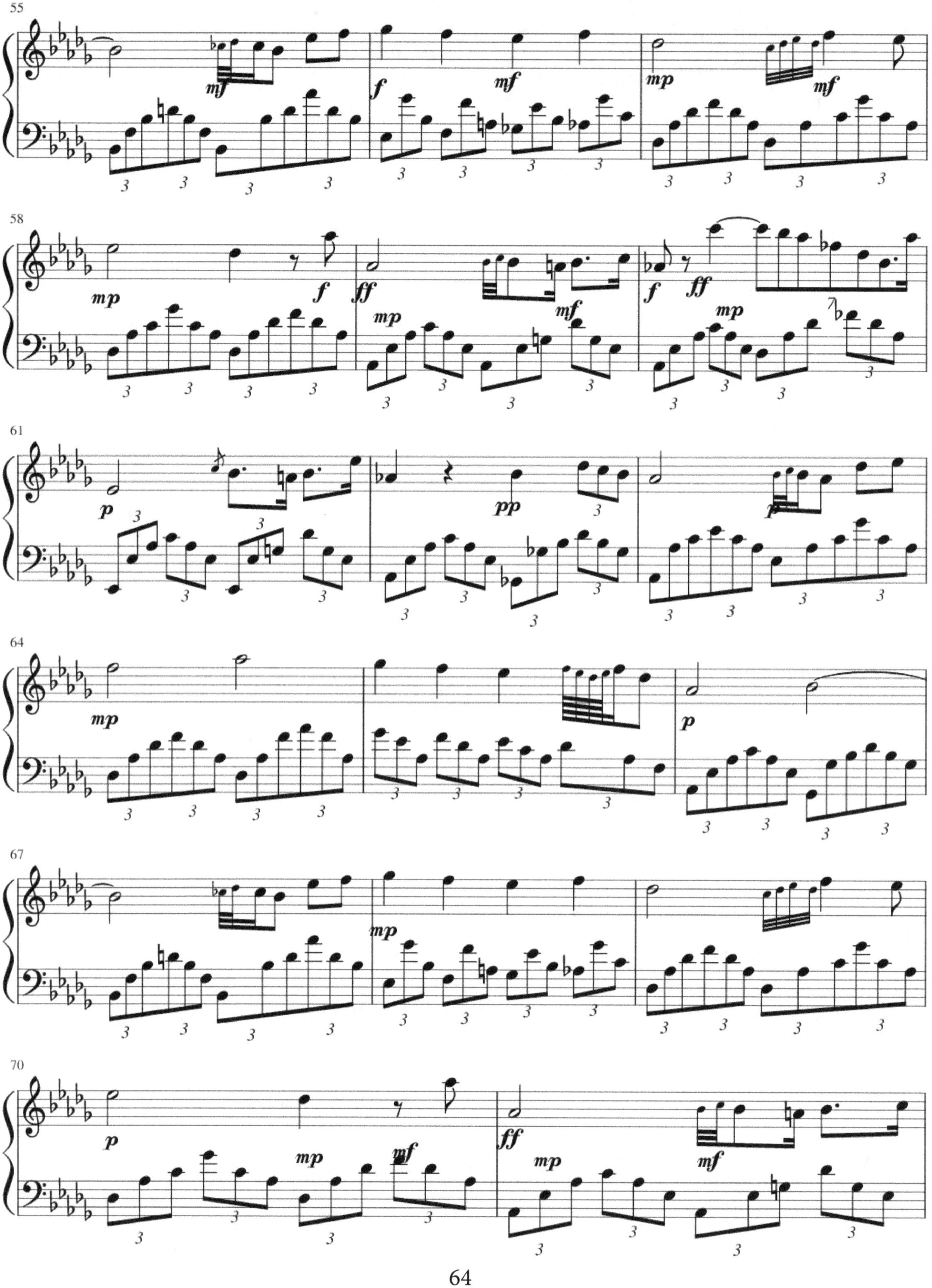
55
58
61
64
67
70

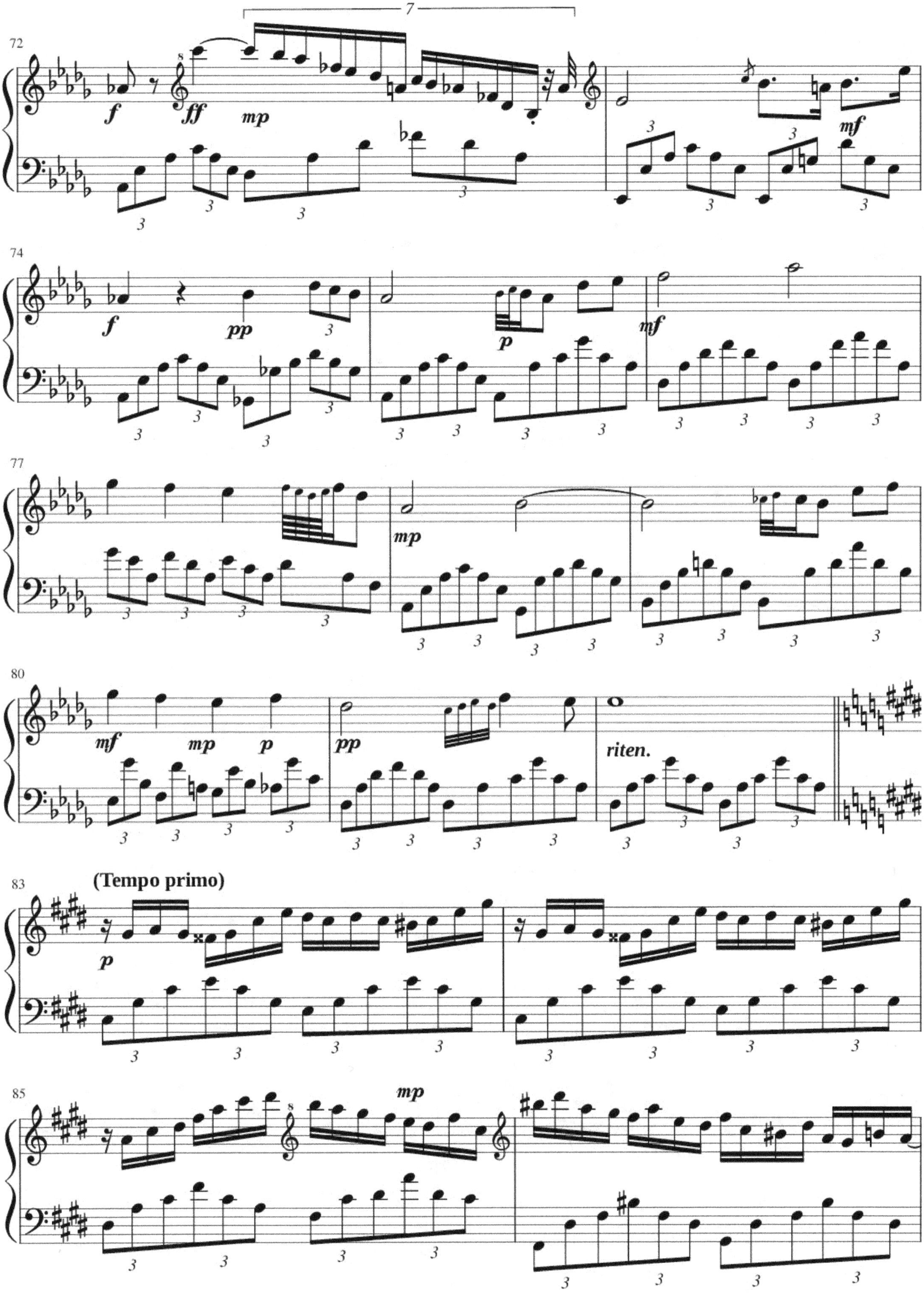
riten.
(Tempo primo)

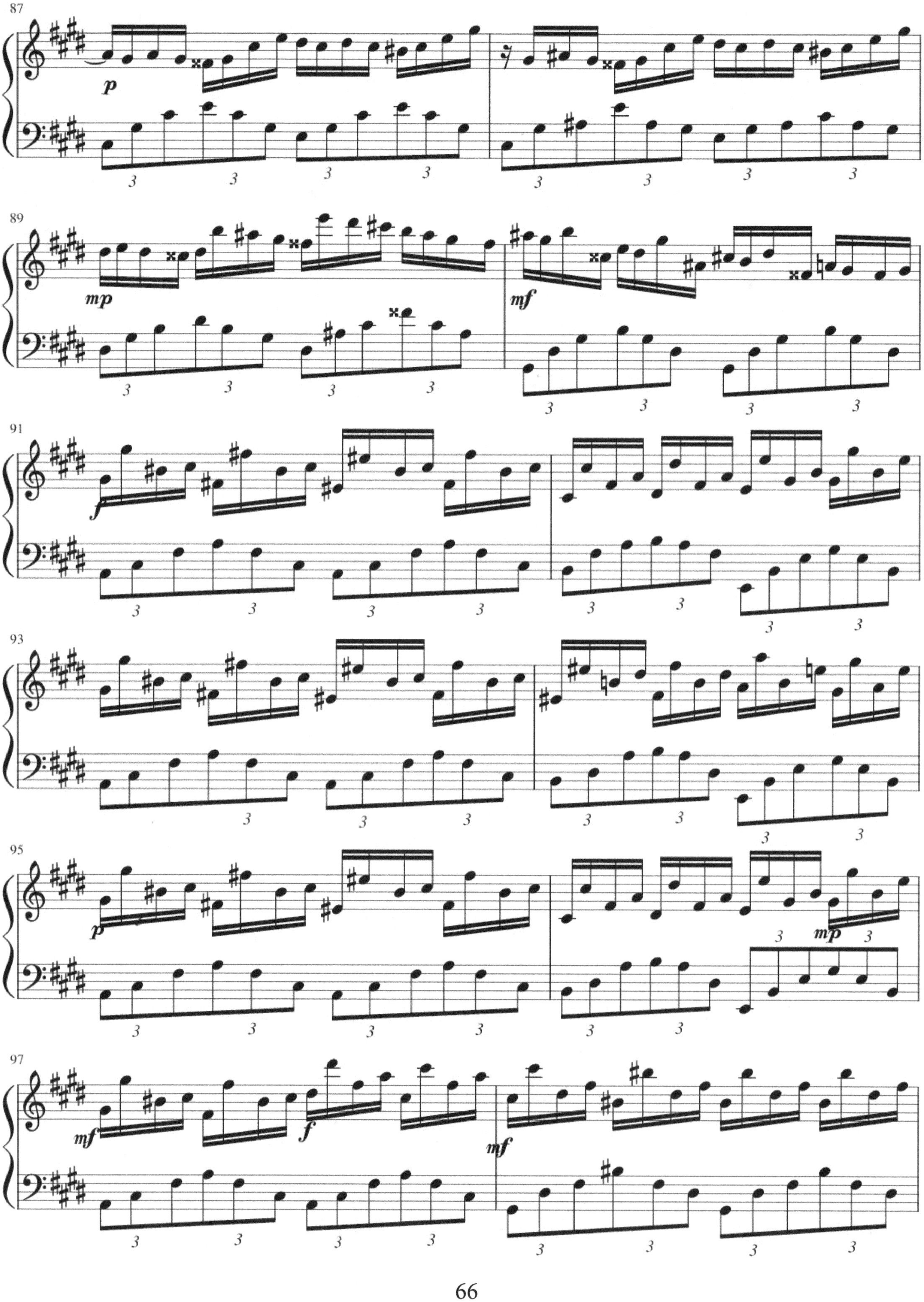
87
p
89
mp
mf
91
f
93
95
p
mp
97
mf
f
mf

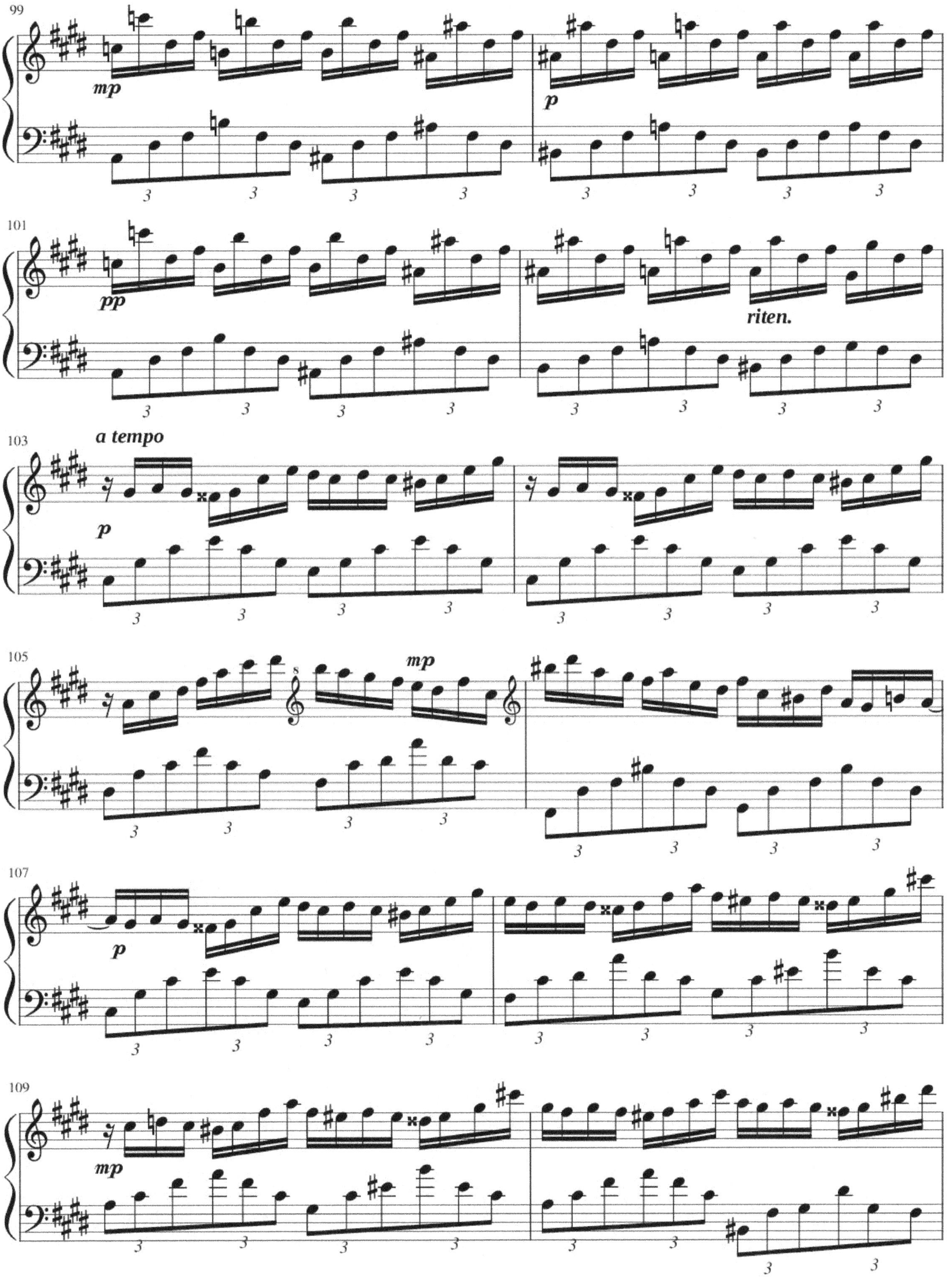
99
mp
p
101
pp
riten.
103
a tempo
p
105
mp
107
p
109
mp

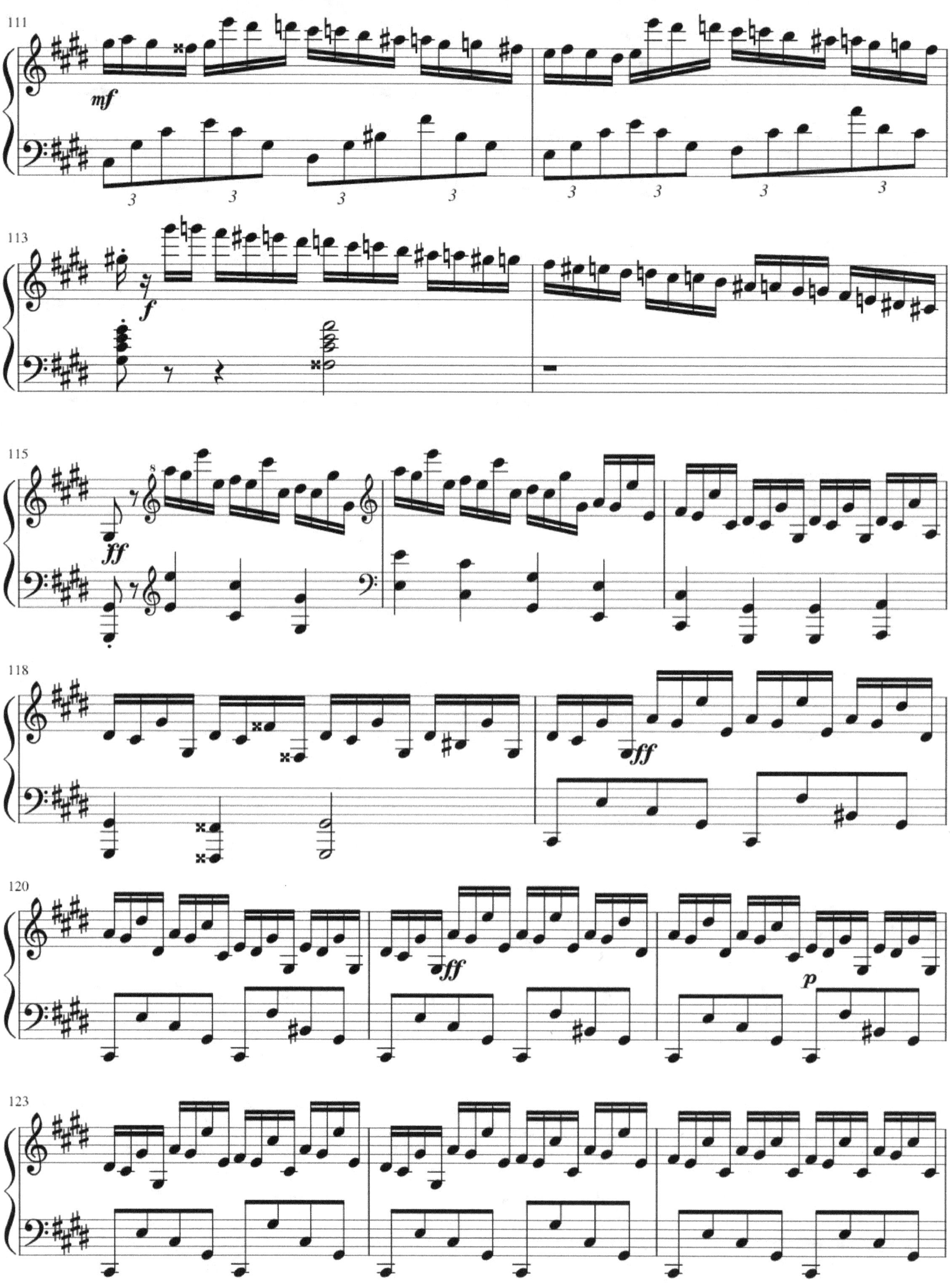
111
mf
113
f
115
ff
118
ff
120
ff
p
123

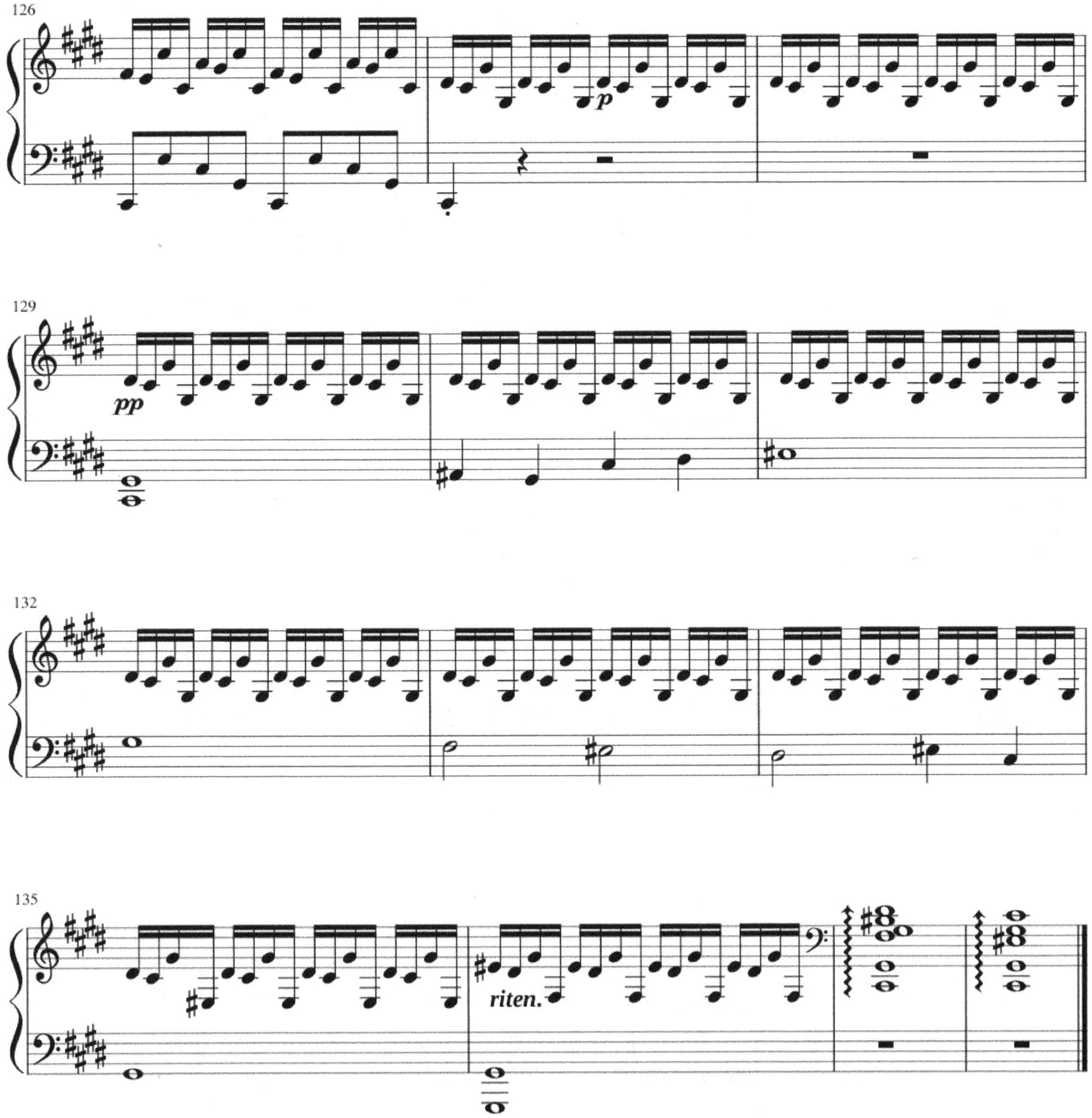
126
p
129
pp
132
135
riten.

Pathetique
Opus No 13

Ludwig Van Beethoven

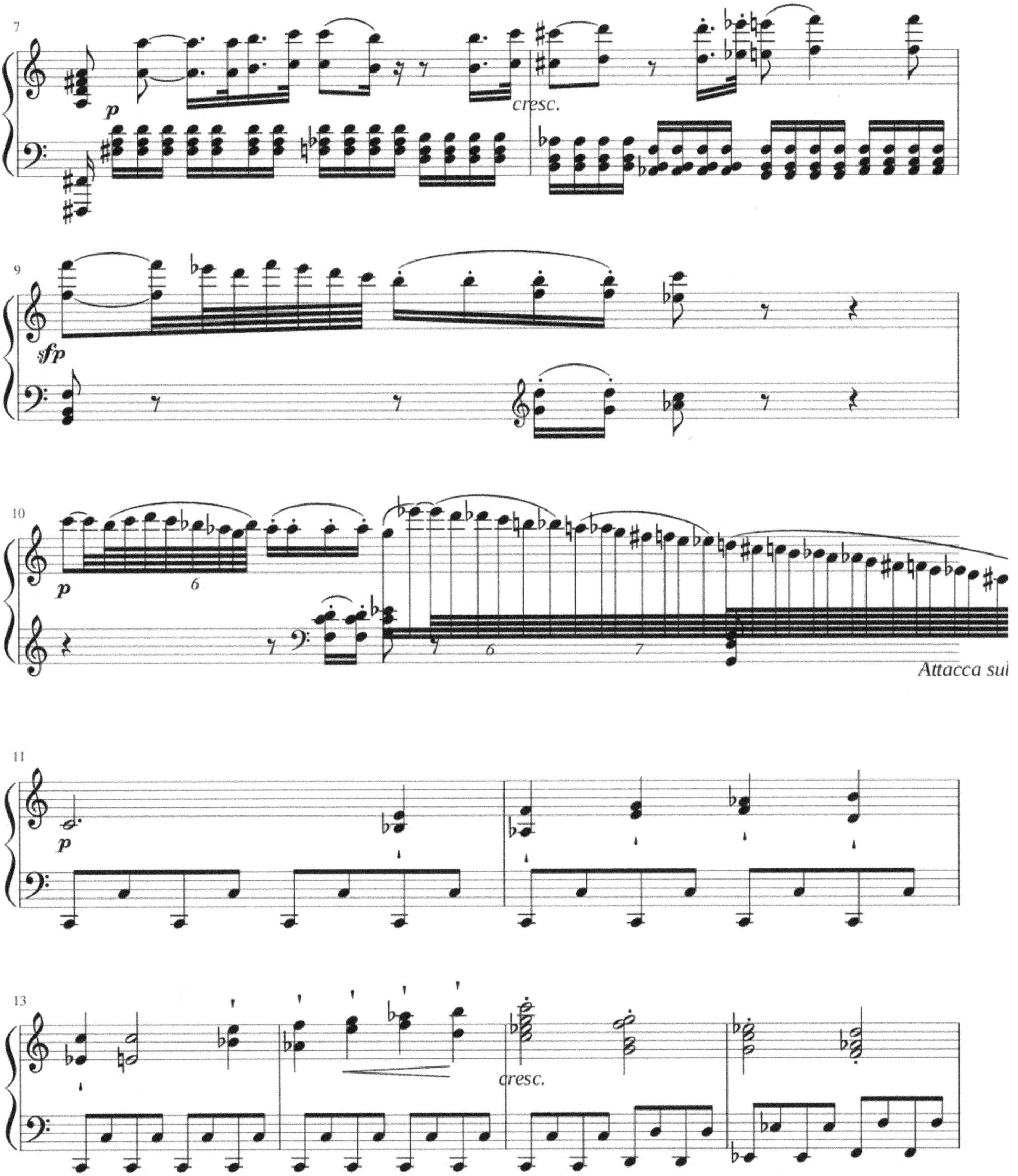

7
p
cresc.
9
sfp
10
p
6
7
Attacca sul
11
p
13
cresc.

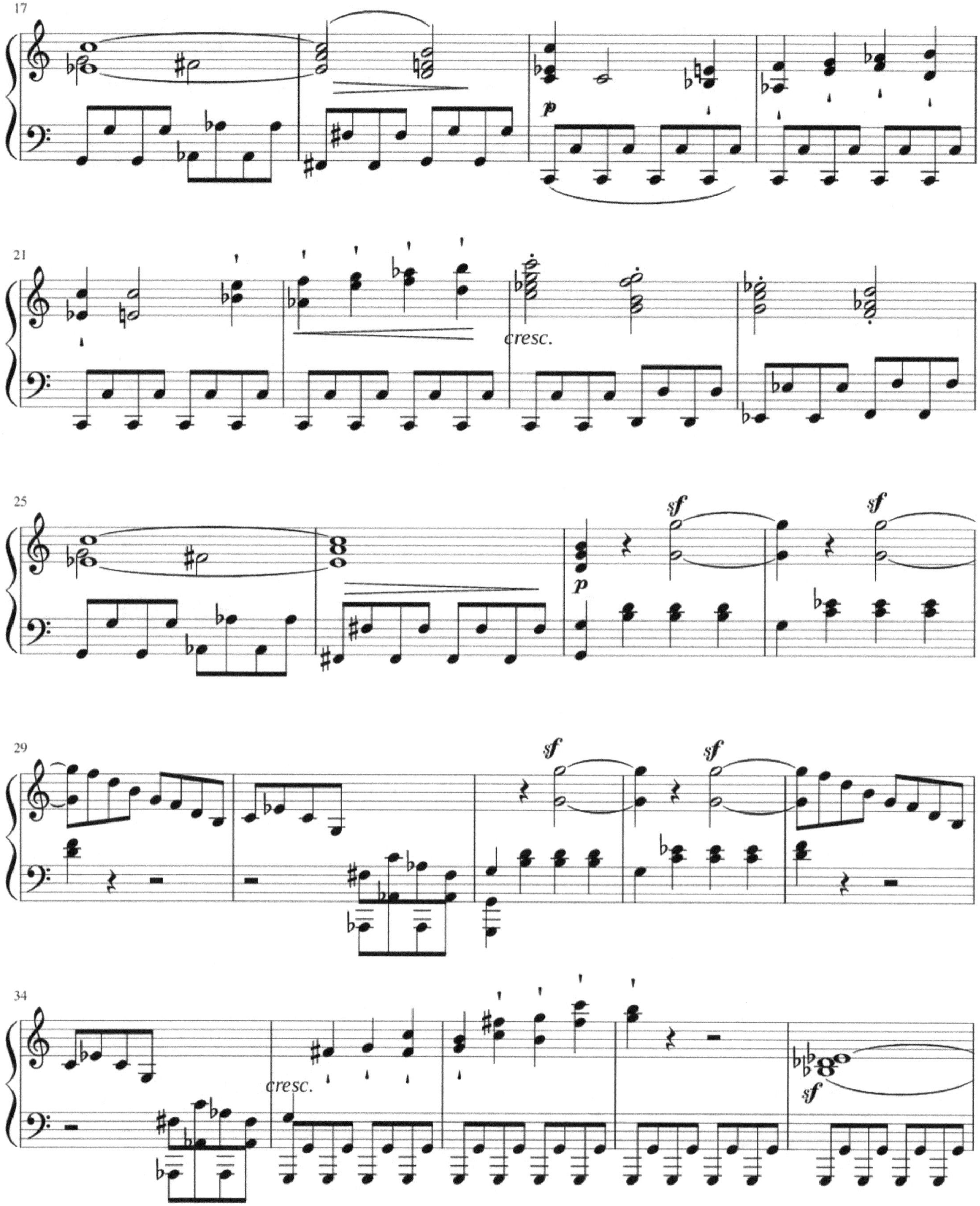
17
p
21
cresc.
25
sf
sf
p
29
sf
sf
34
cresc.
sf

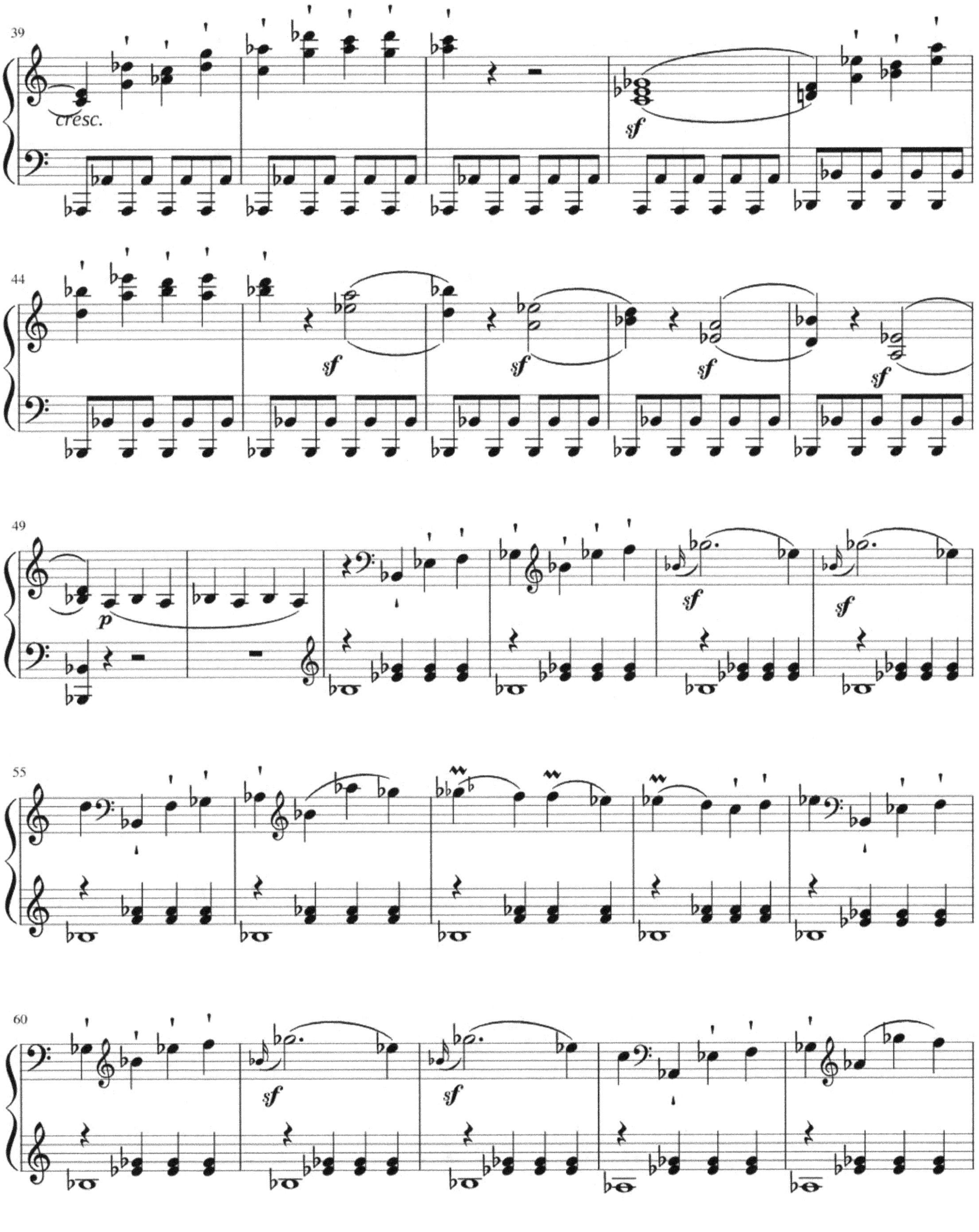

39
cresc.
sf
44
sf
sf
sf
sf
49
p
sf
sf
55
60
sf
sf

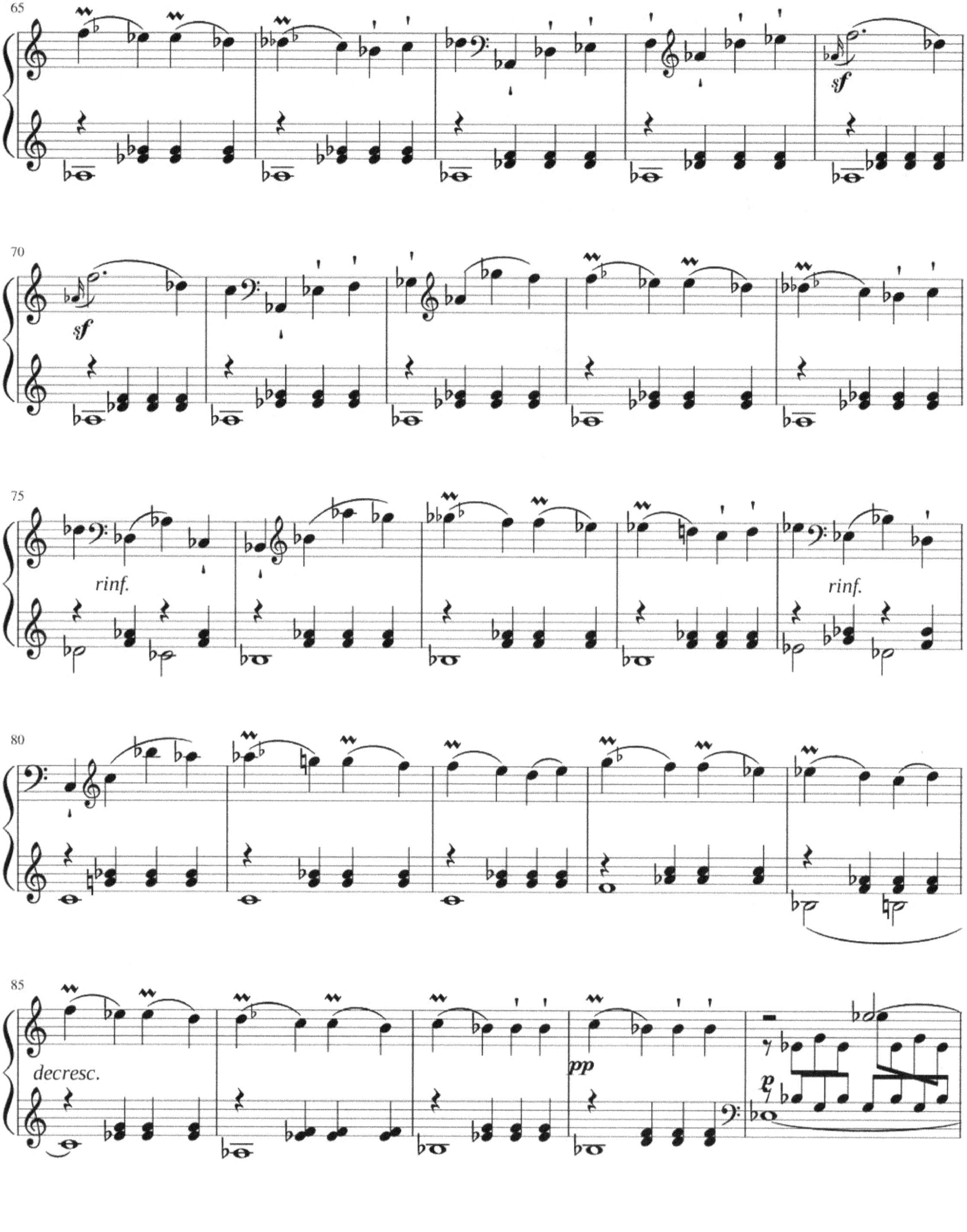
65
sf
70
sf
75
rinf.
rinf.
80
85
decresc.
pp
p

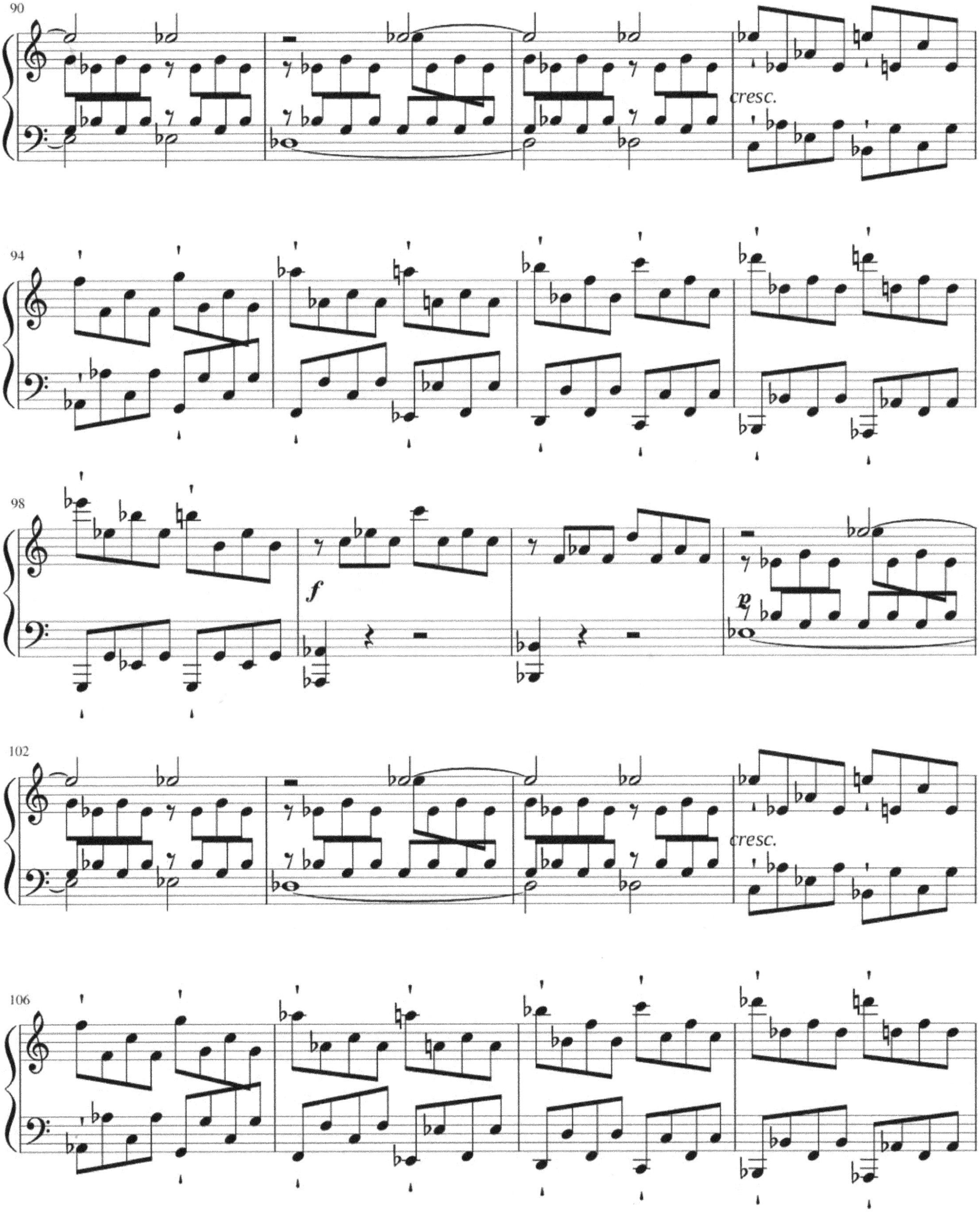
90
cresc.
94
98
f
p
102
cresc.
106

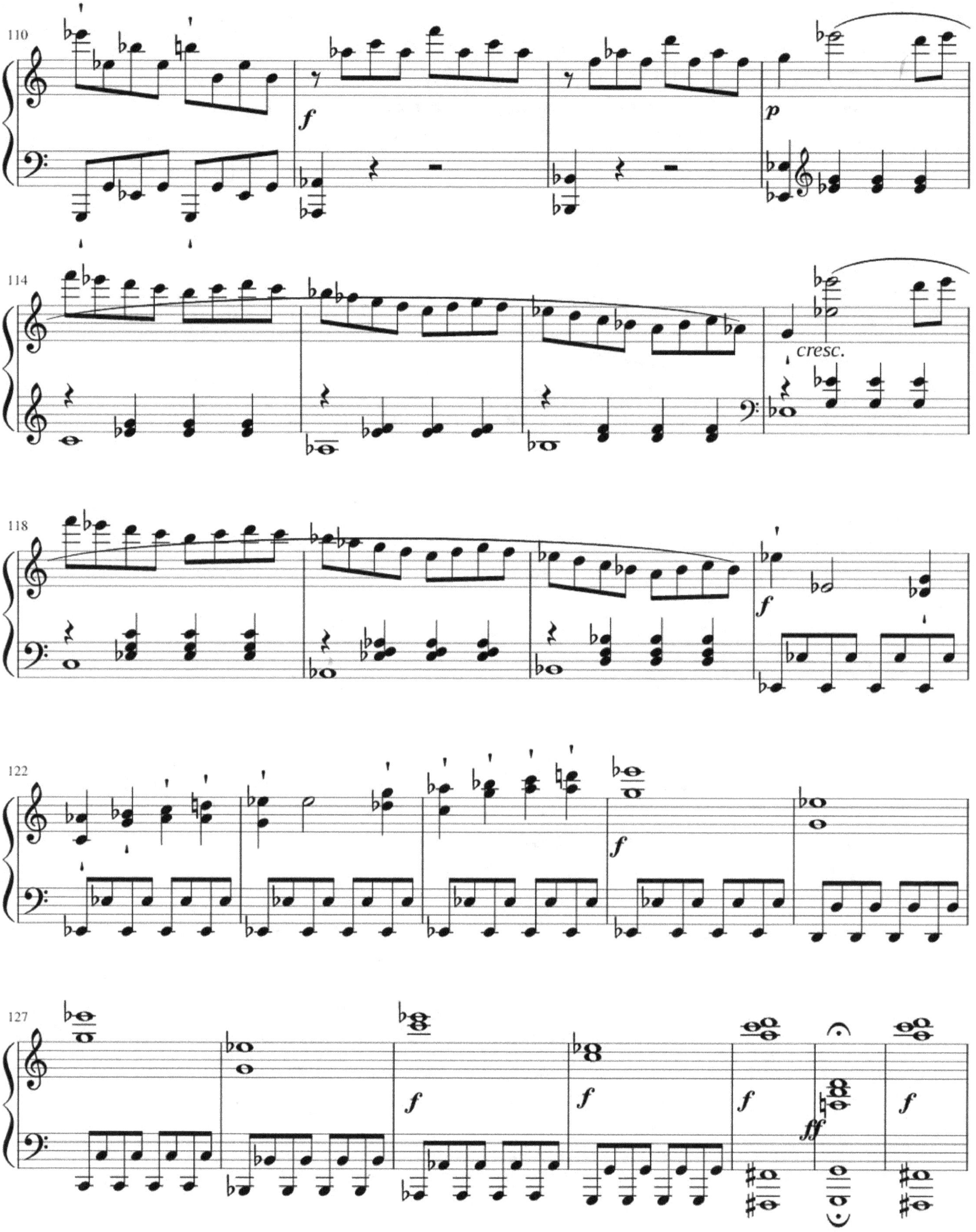
110
f
p
114
cresc.
118
f
122
f
127
f
f
f
ff
f

134
ff
fp
fp
fp
p
138
decresc.
pp
p cresc.
f
p
144
cresc.
f
p
150
cresc.
155

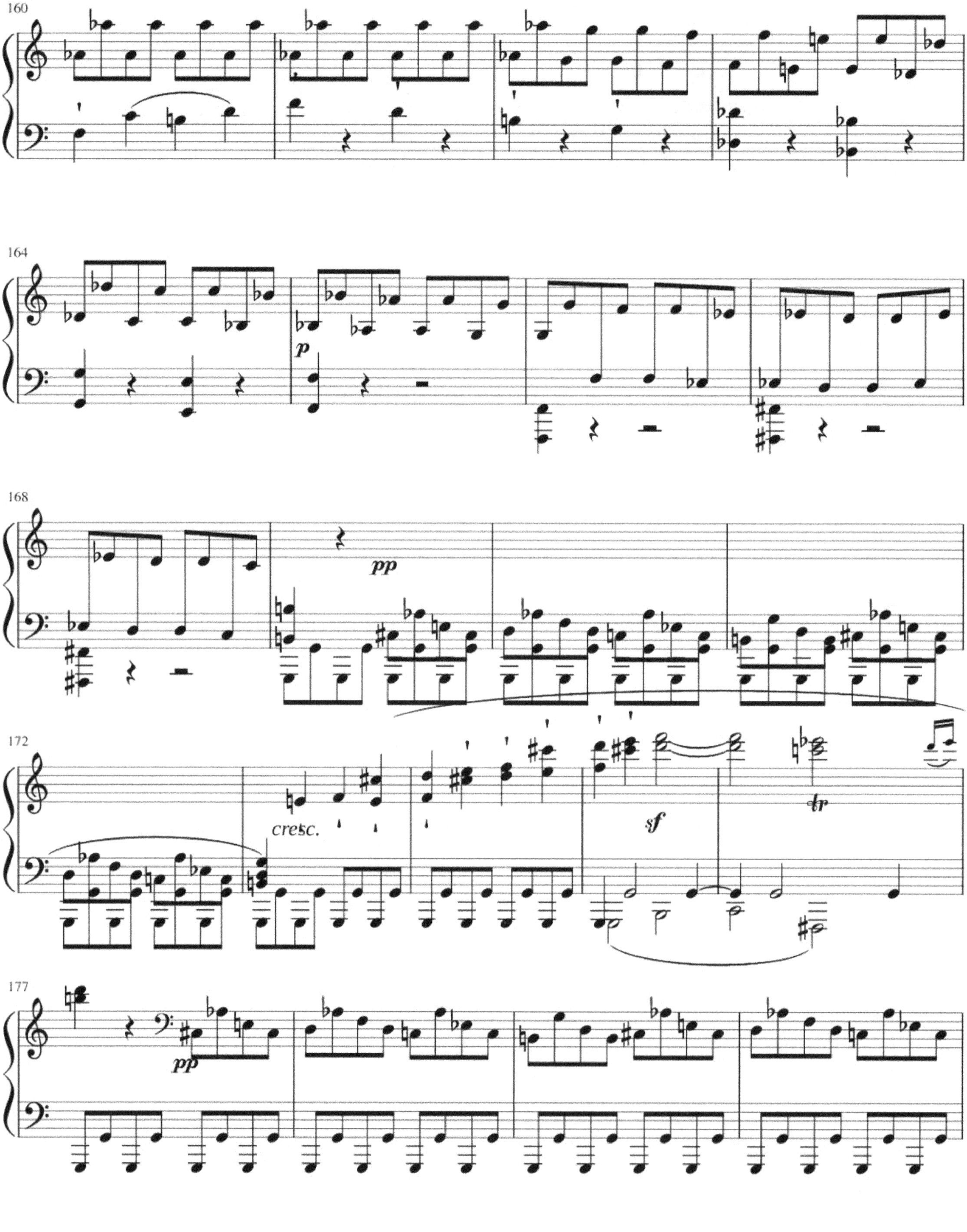
160
164
p
168
pp
172
cresc.
sf
tr
177
pp

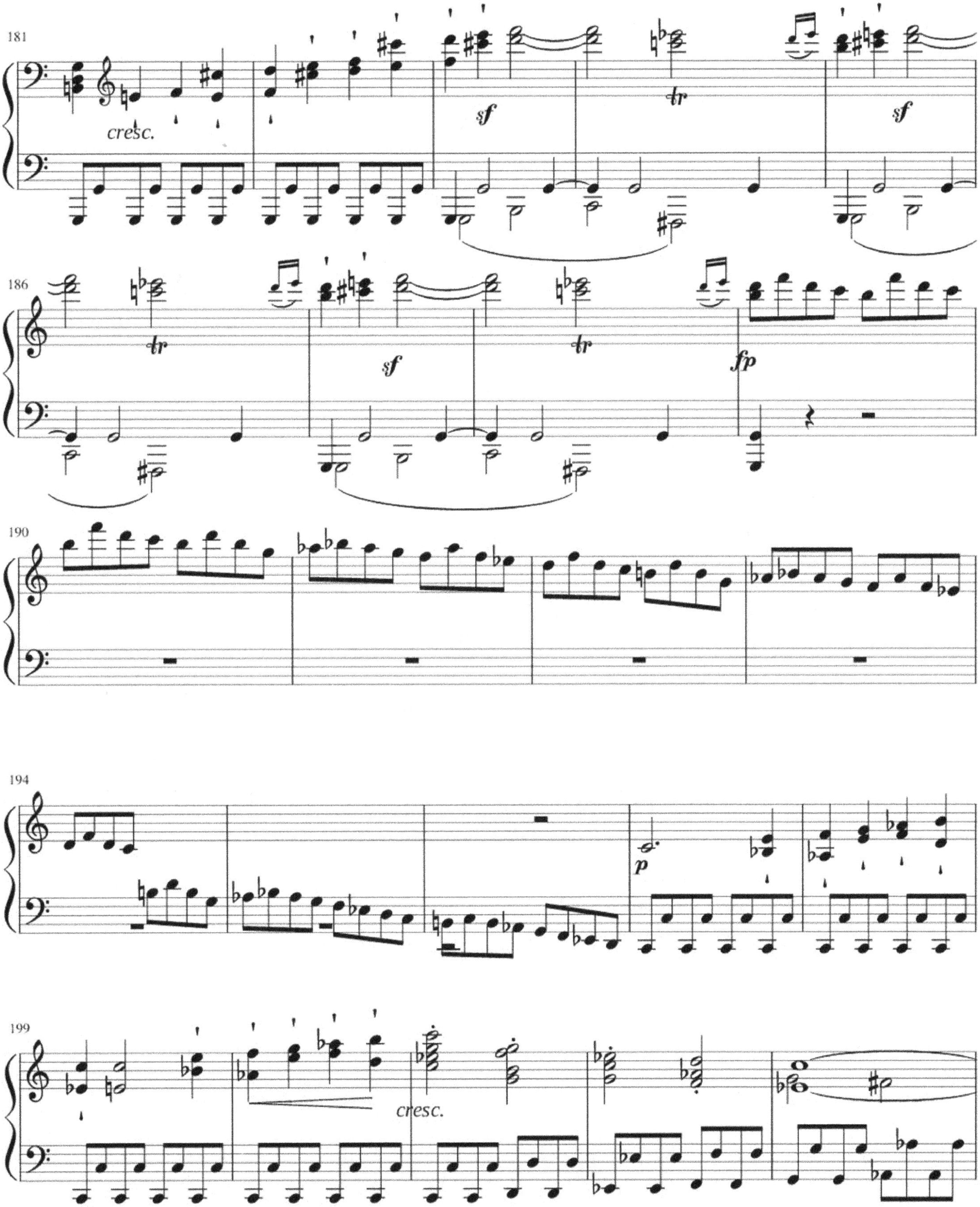
181
cresc.
sf
tr
sf
186
tr
sf
tr
fp
190
194
p
199
cresc.

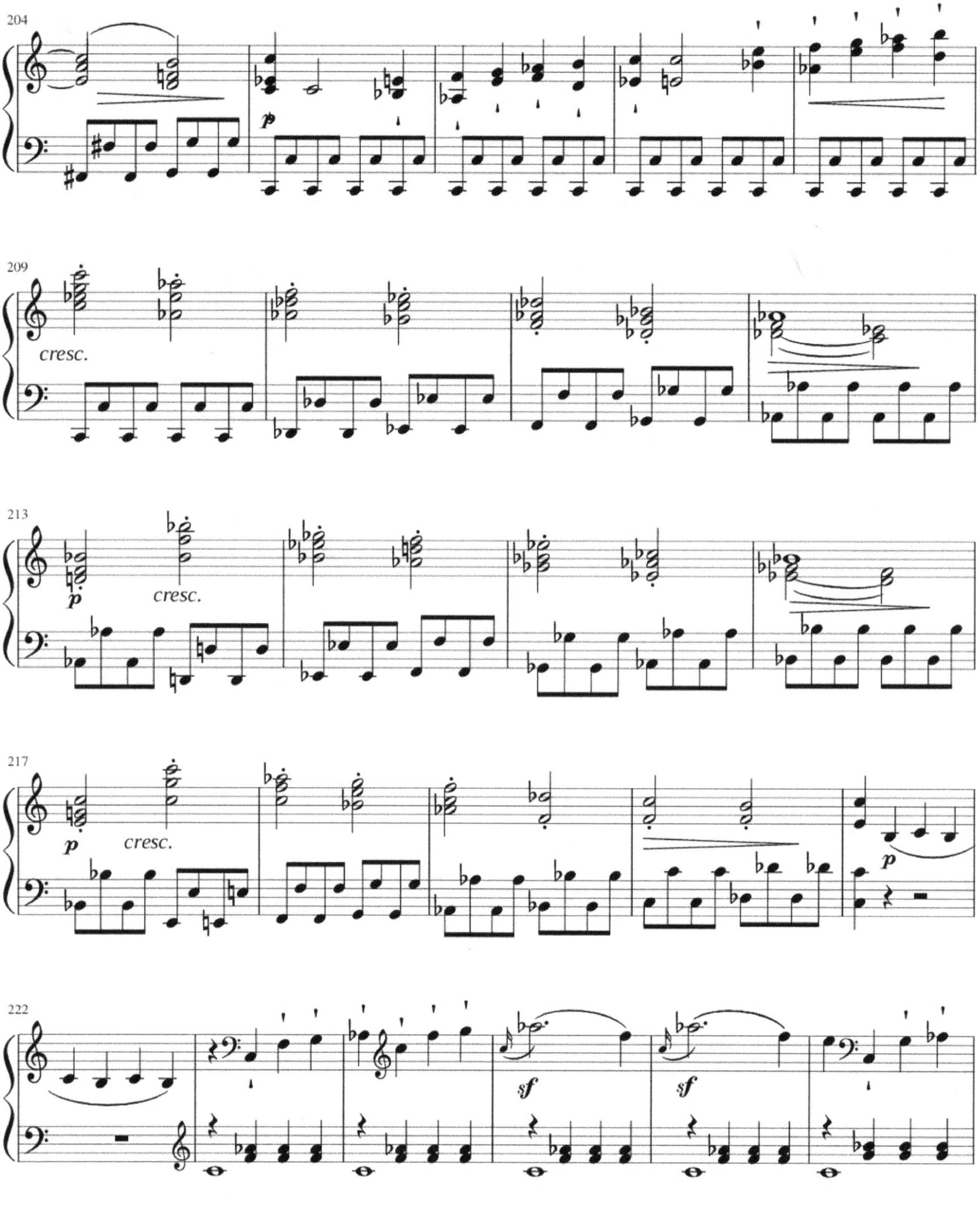
204
p
209
cresc.
213
p
cresc.
217
p
cresc.
p
222
sf
sf

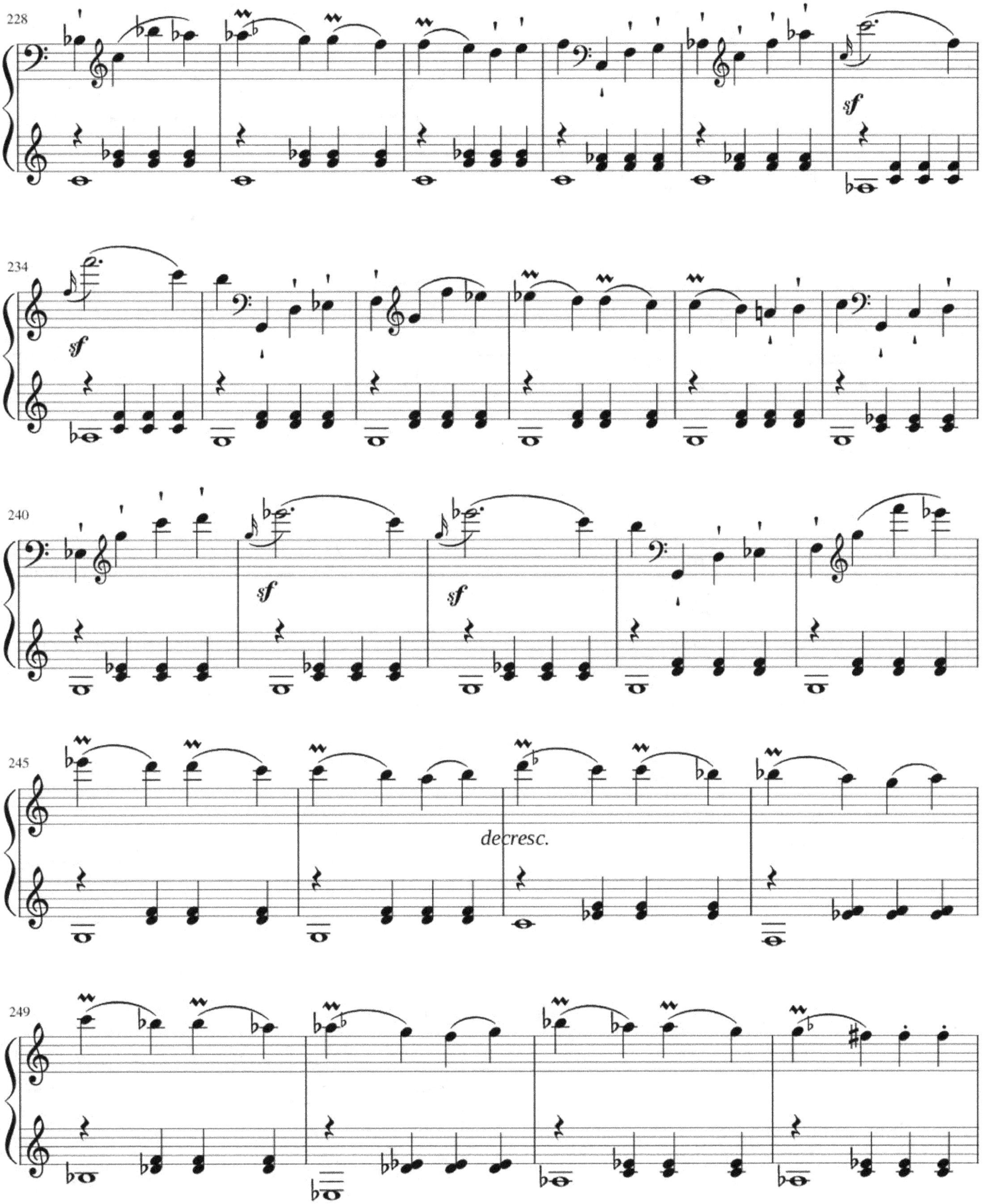
228
sf
234
sf
240
sf
sf
245
decresc.
249

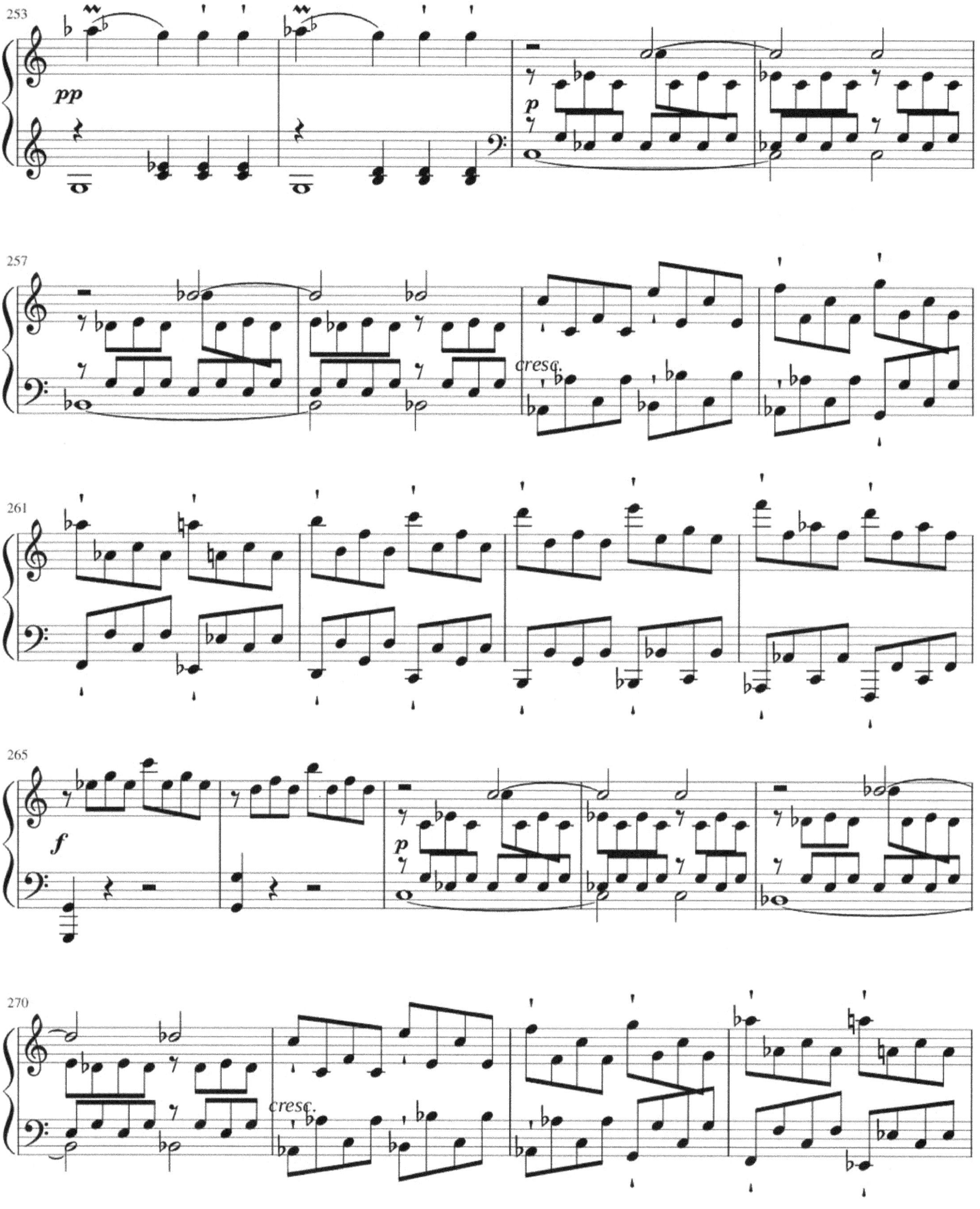
253
pp
p
257
cresc.
261
265
f
p
270
cresc.

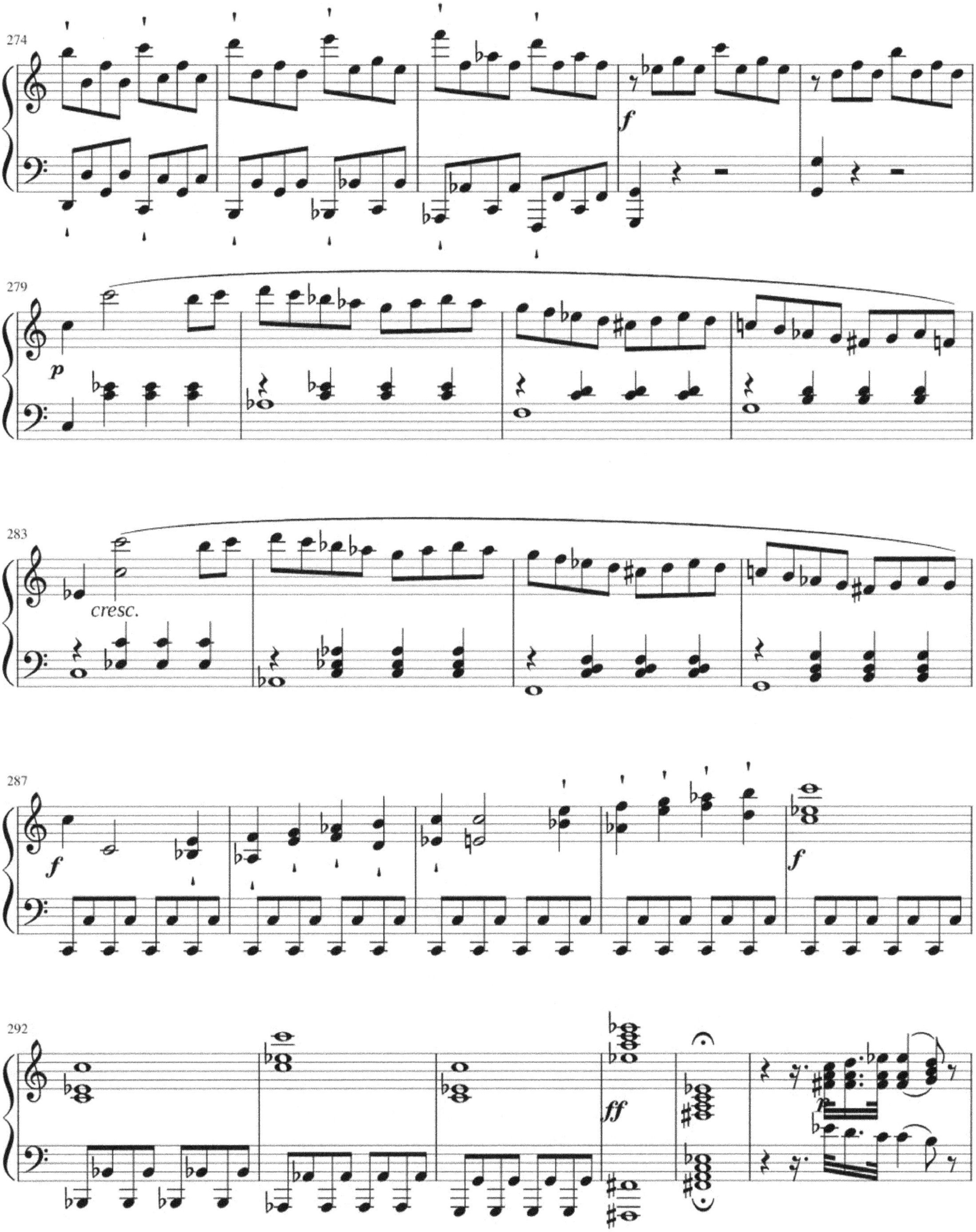
274
f
279
p
283
cresc.
287
f
f
292
ff

298
cresc.
fz
decresc.
pp
301
p
cresc.
306
f
ff
Adagio cantabile
313
314

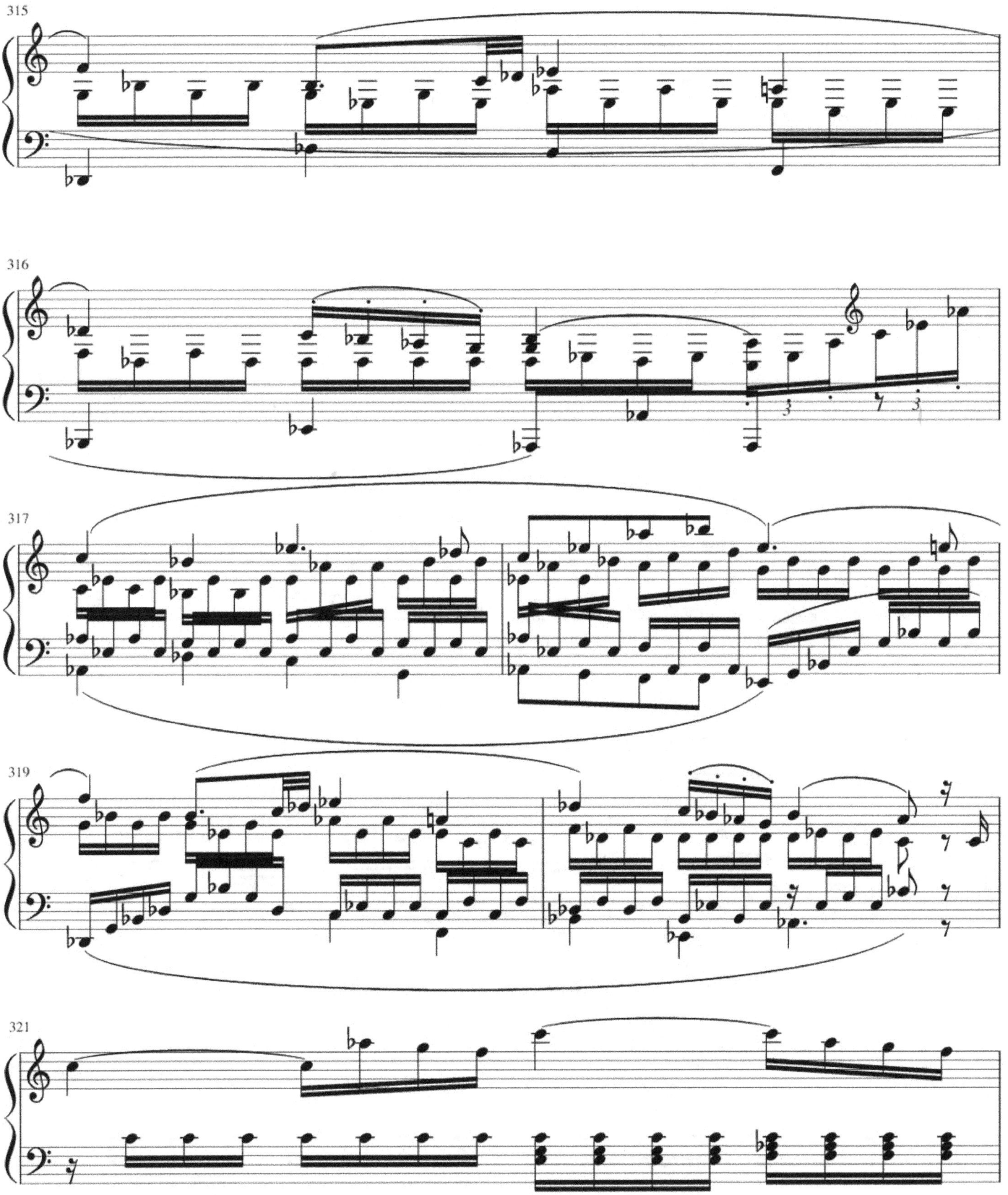
315
316
317
319
321

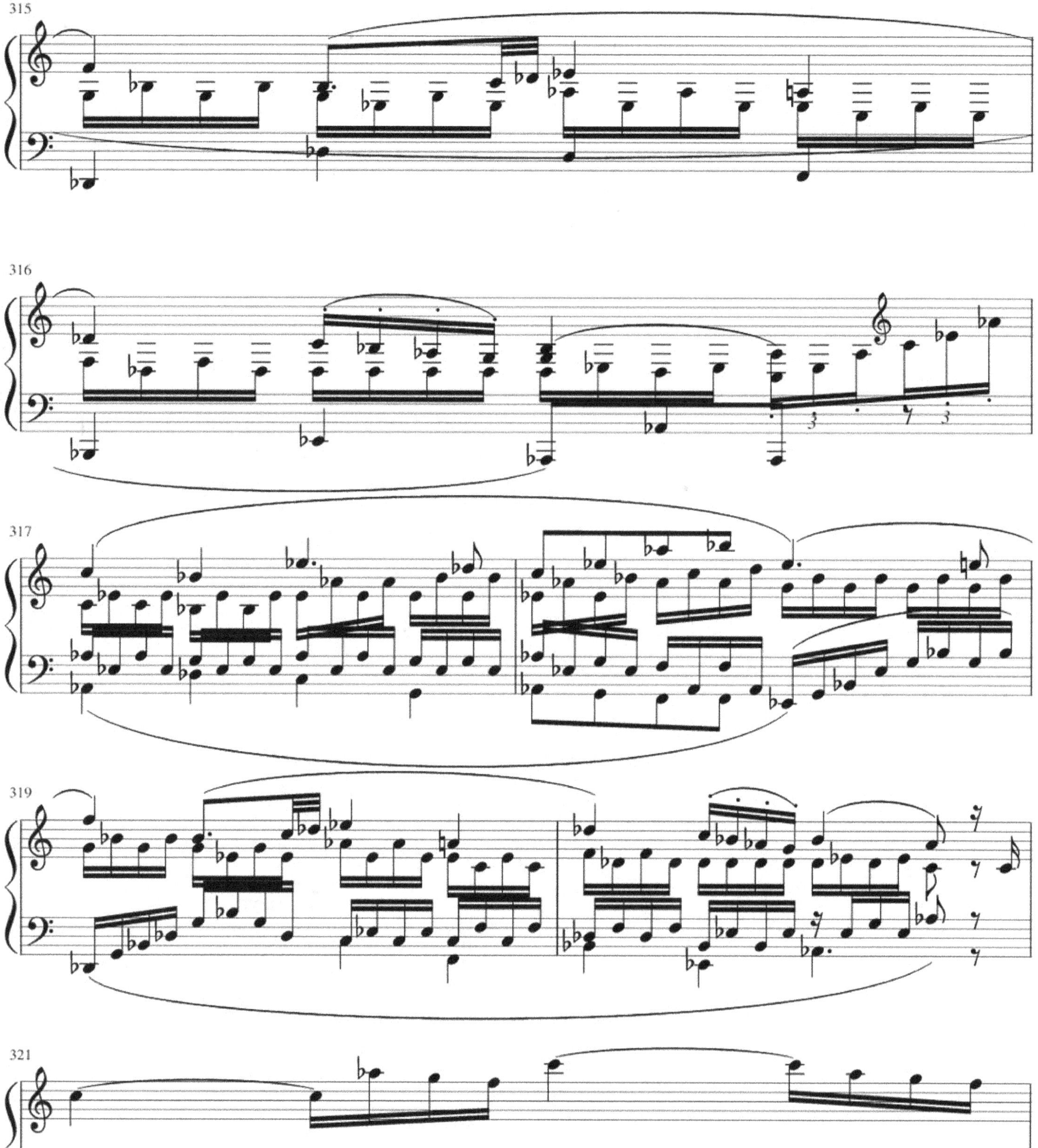
315
316
317
319
321

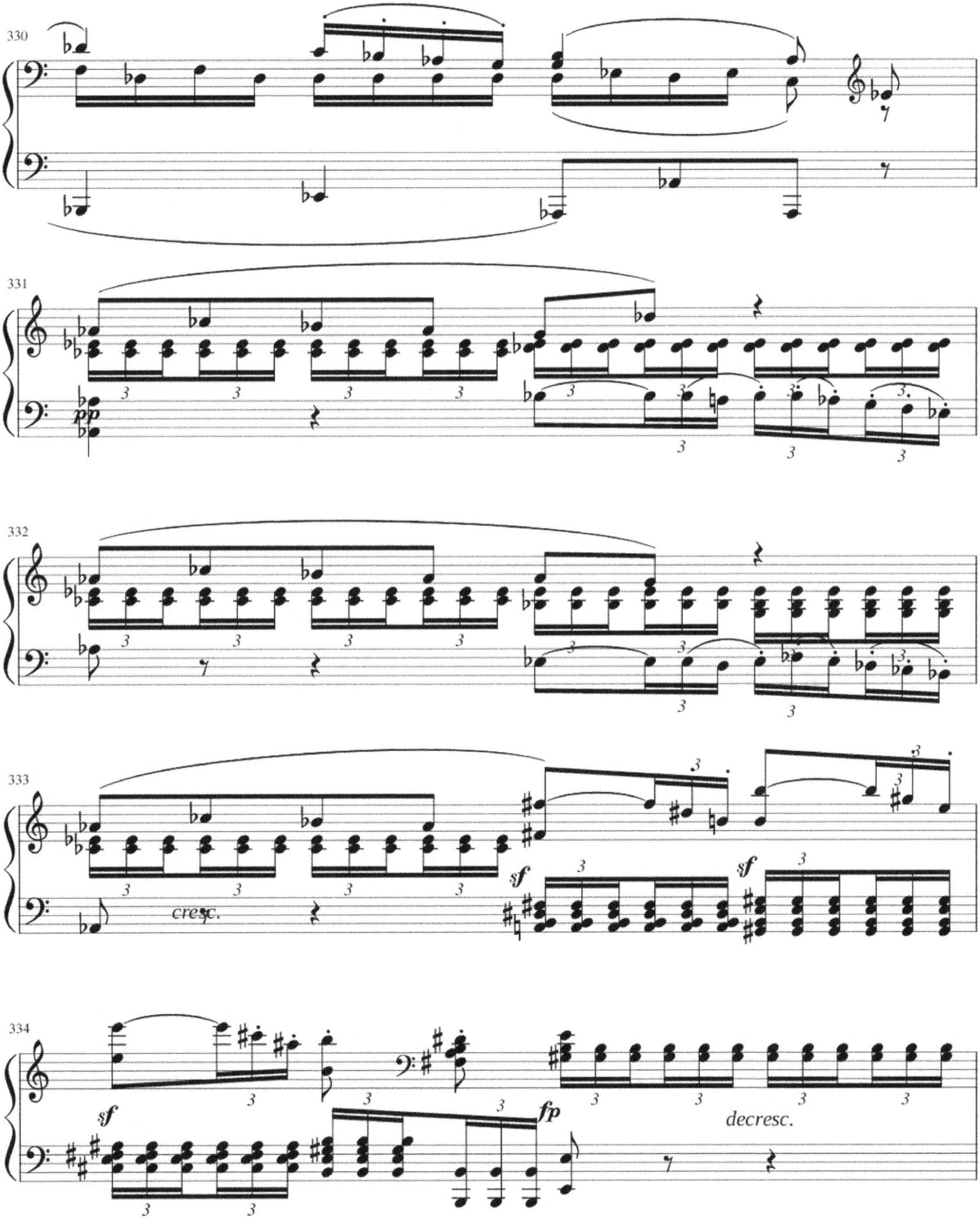
330
331
pp
332
333
cresc.
sf
sf
334
sf
fp
decresc.

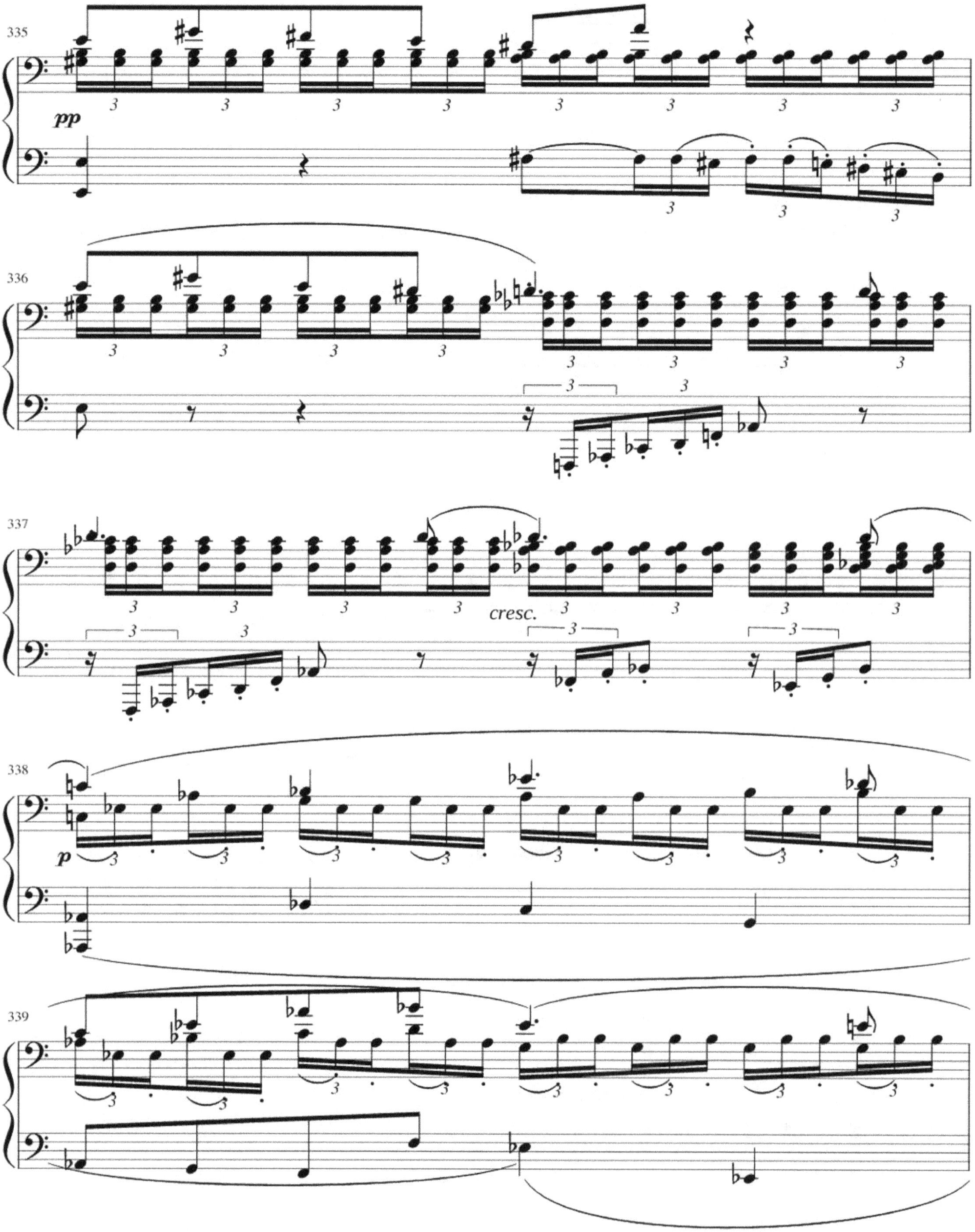
335
pp
336
337
cresc.
338
p
339

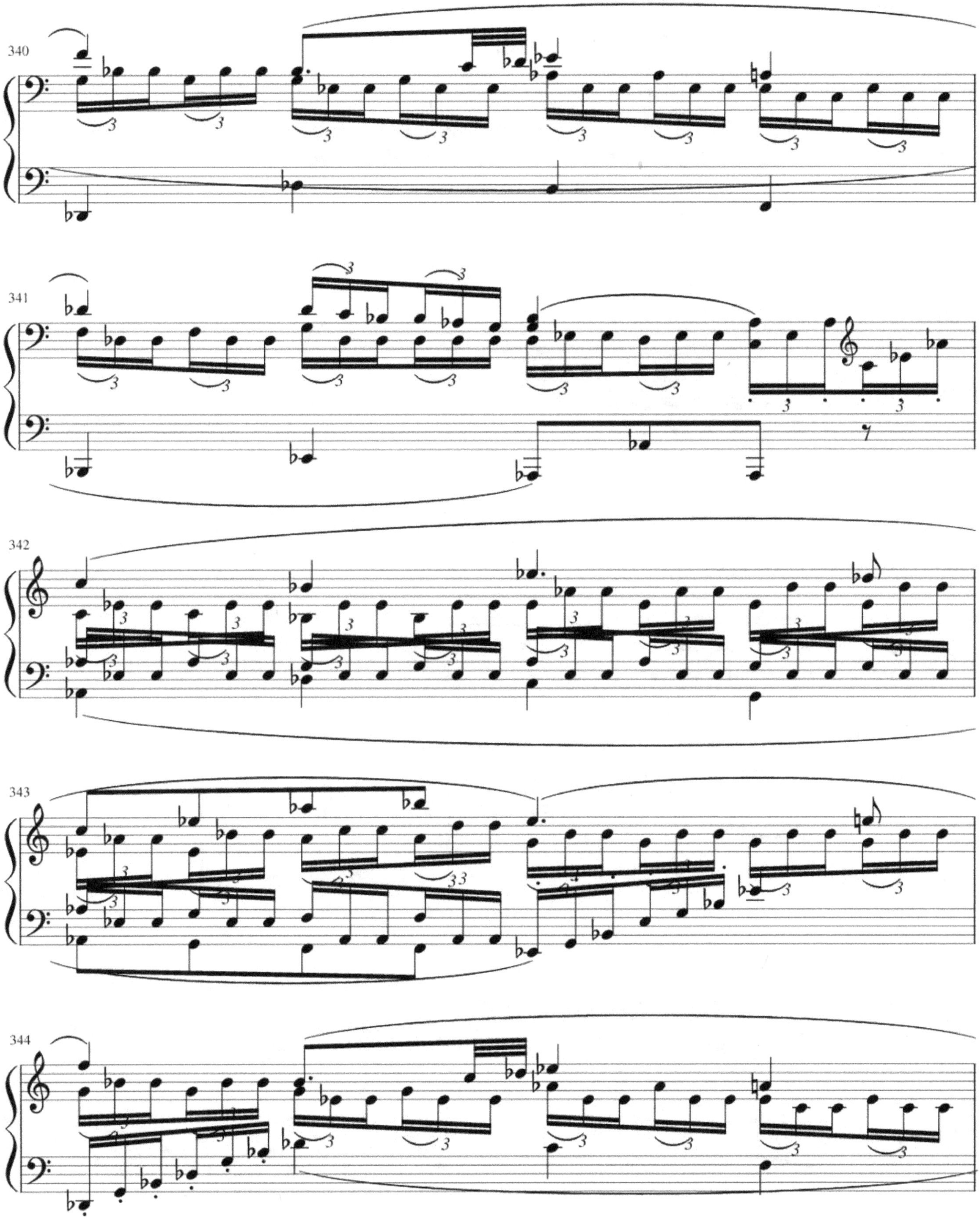
340
341
342
343
344

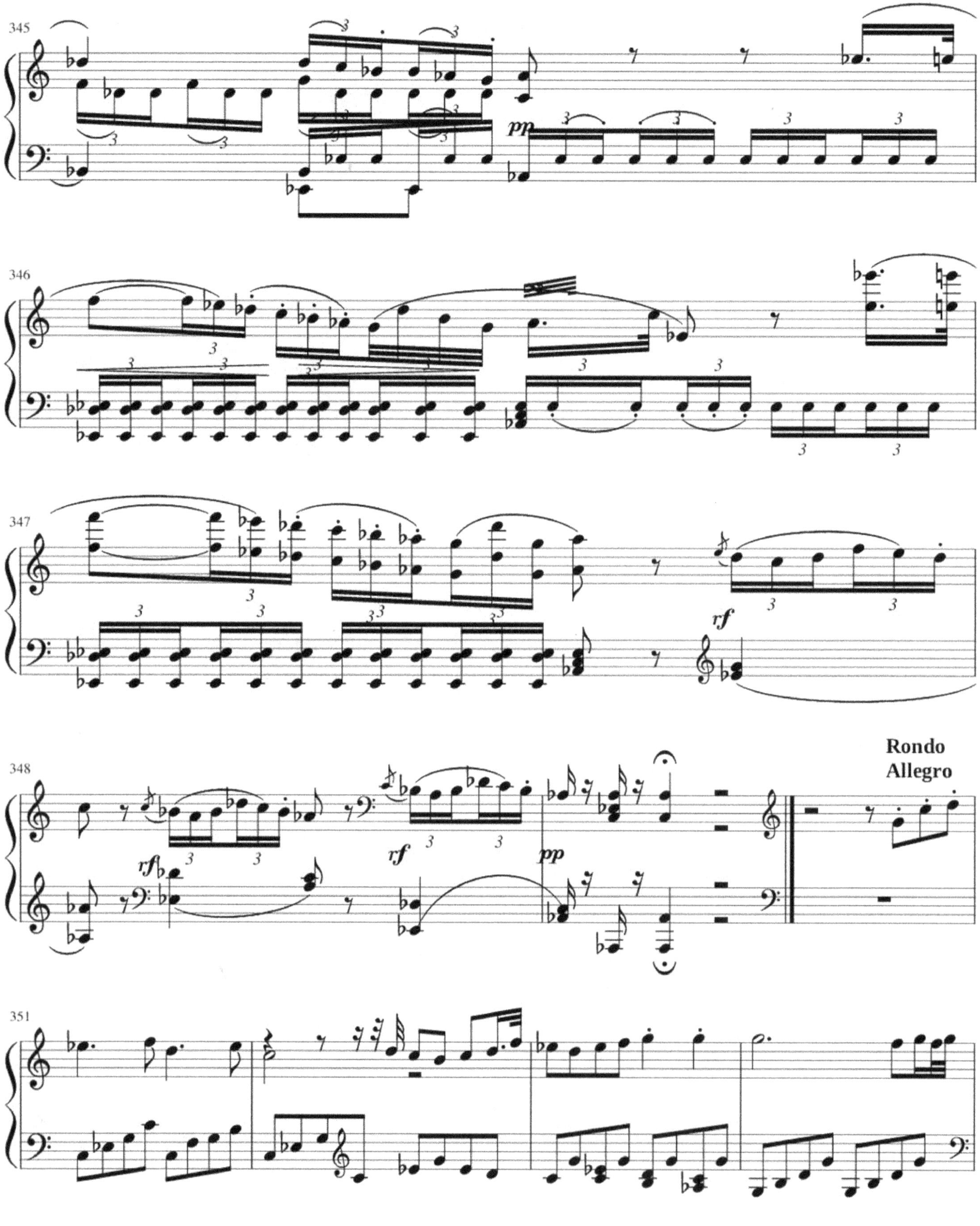
345
pp
346
347
rf
348
rf
rf
pp
Rondo
Allegro
351

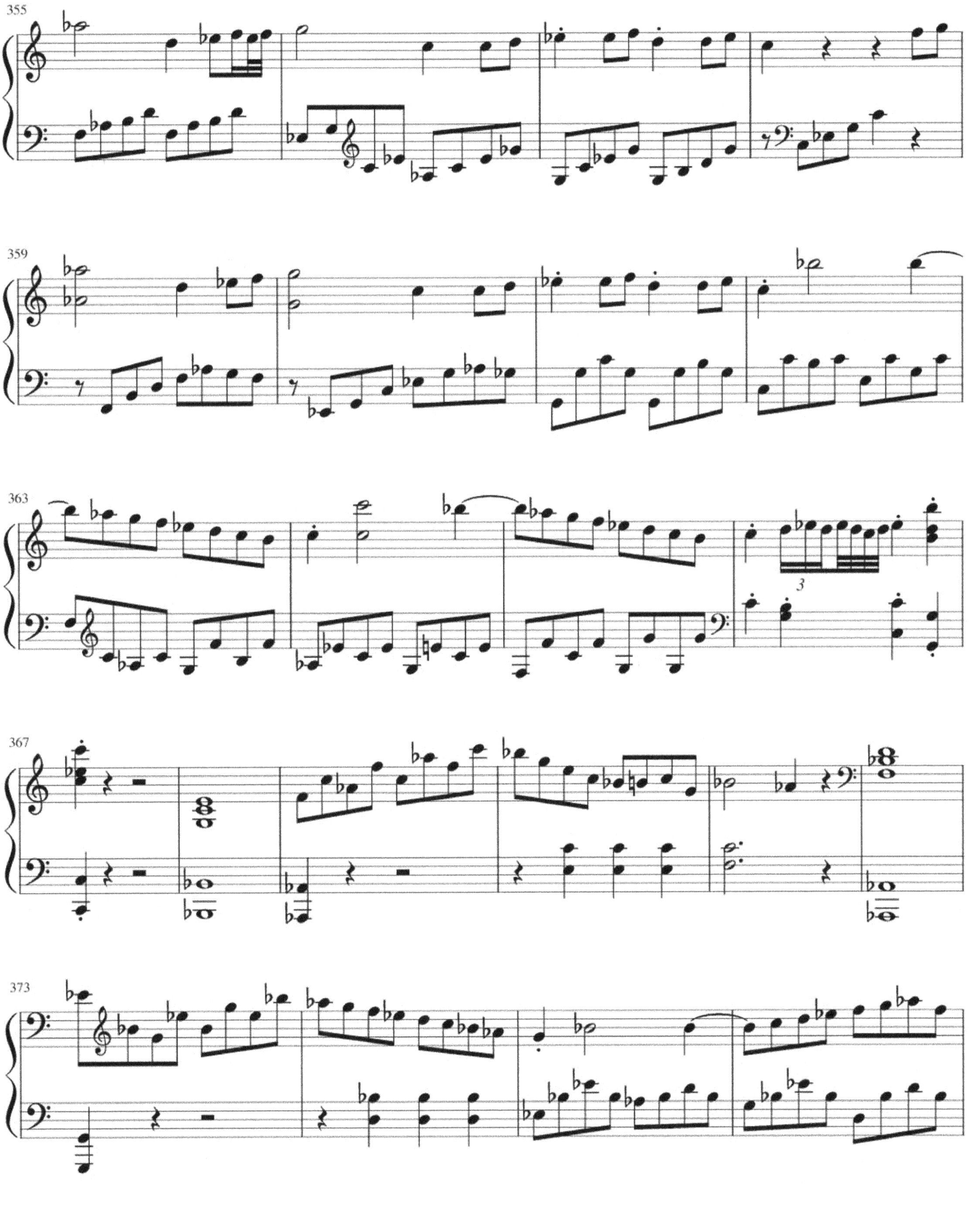
355
359
363
3
367
373

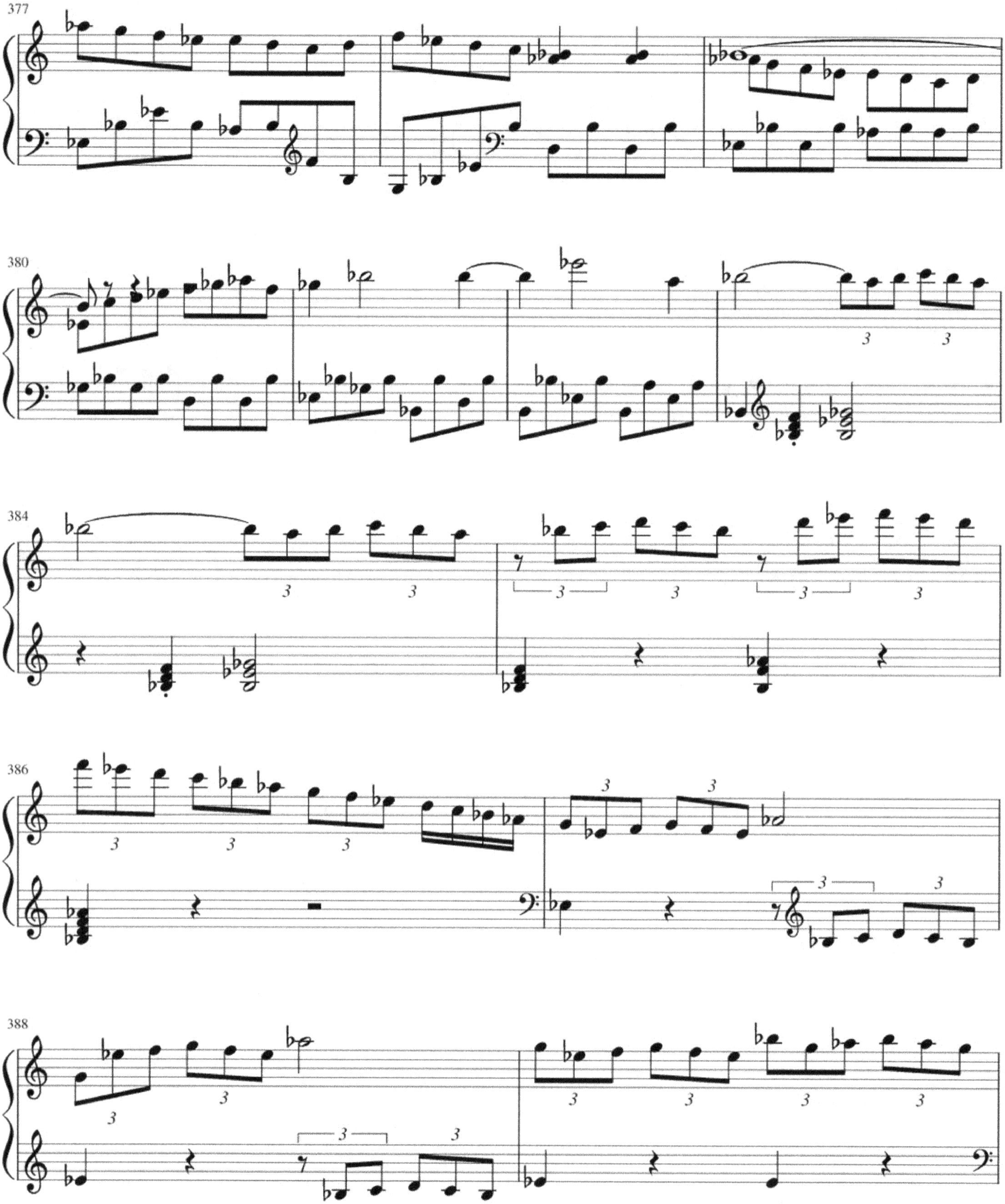
377
380
384
386
388

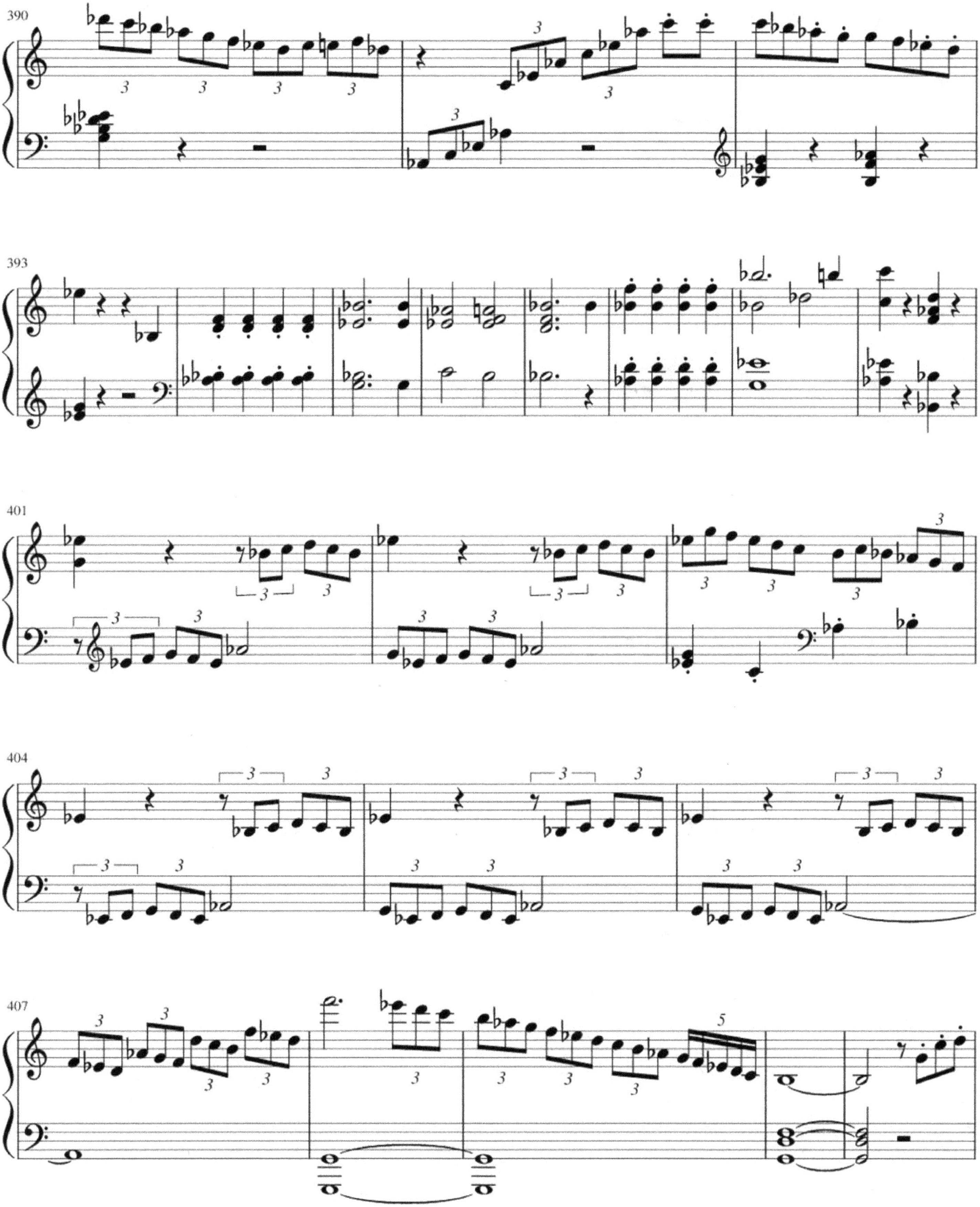
390
393
401
404
407

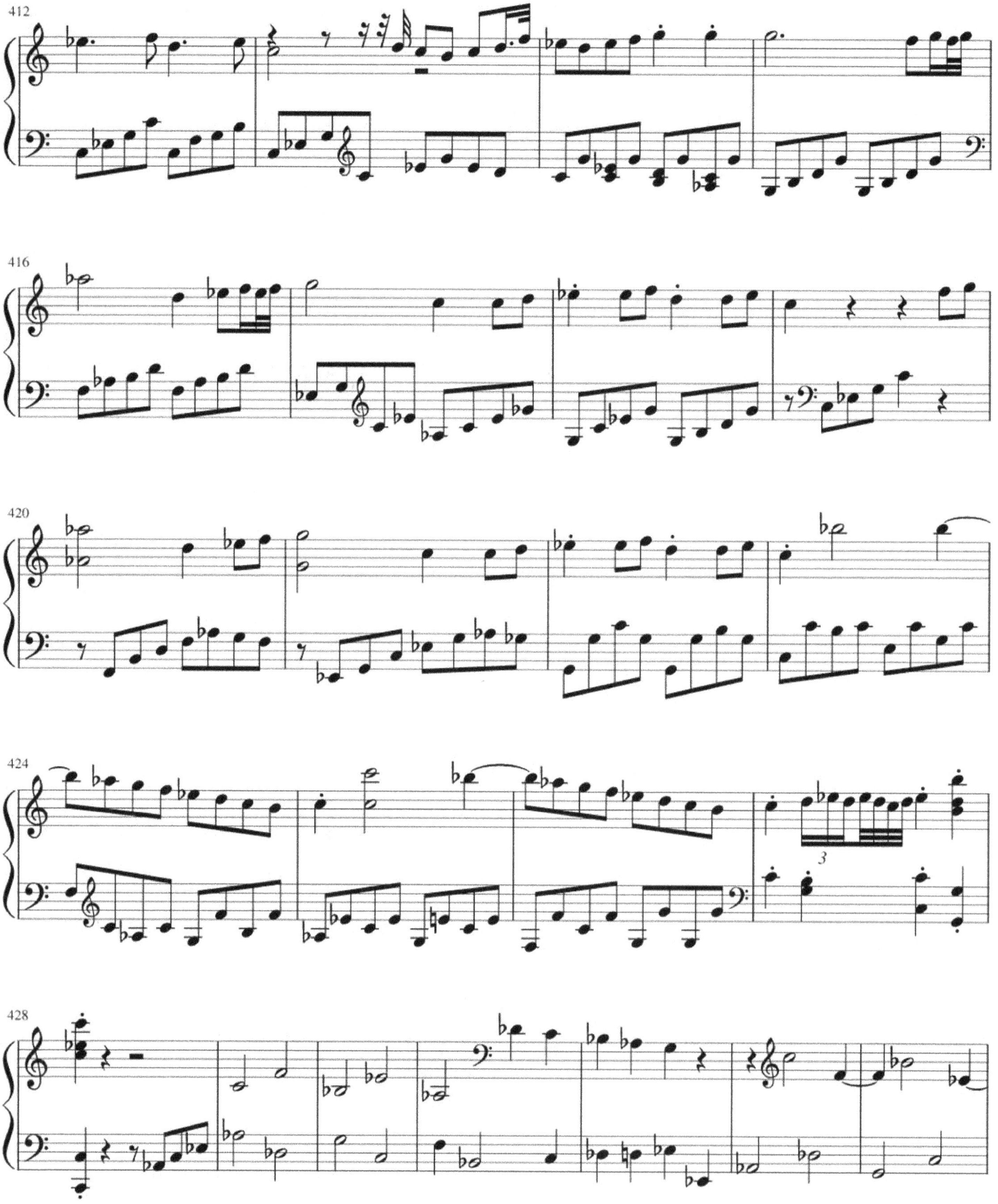
412
416
420
424
3
428

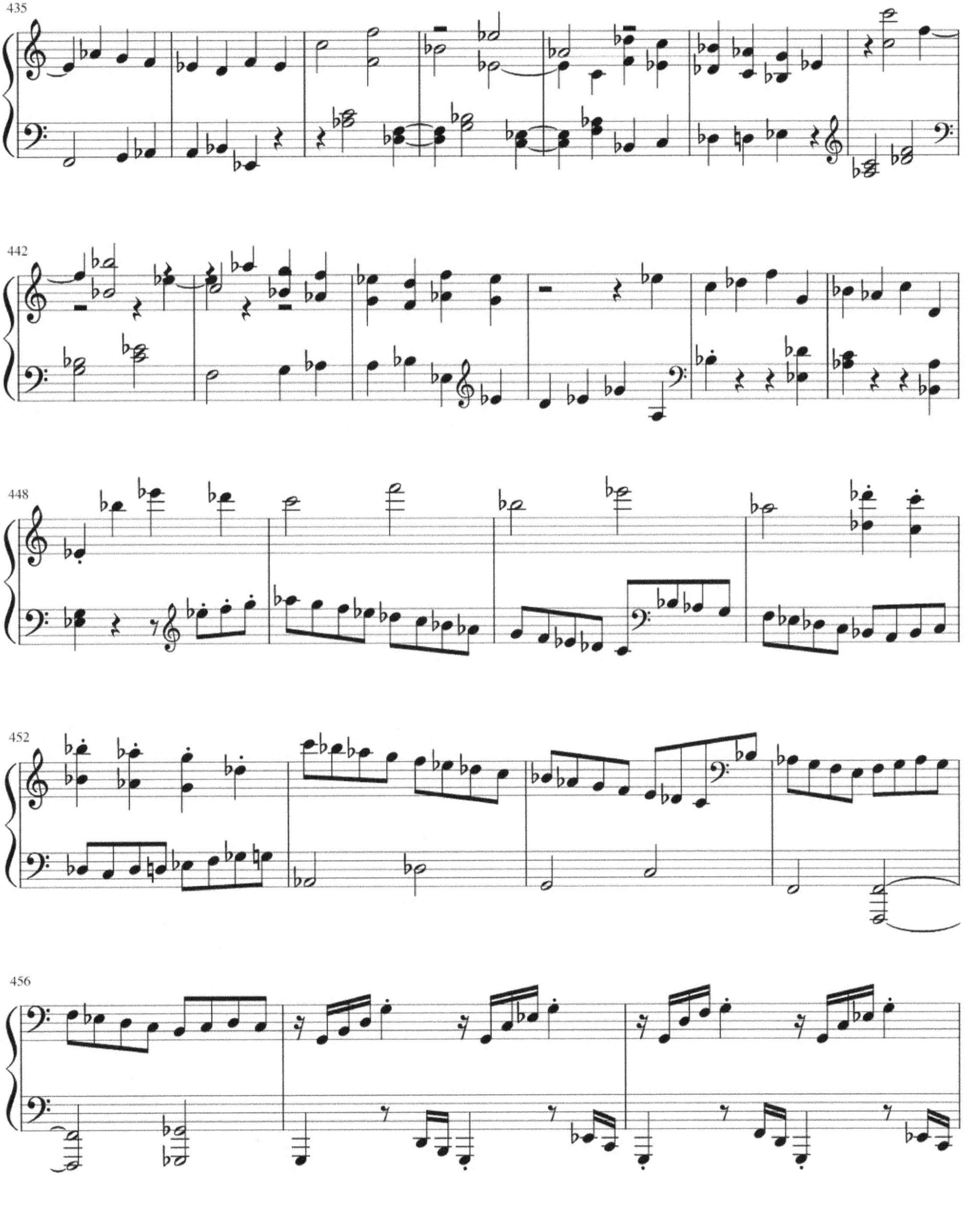
435
442
448
452
456

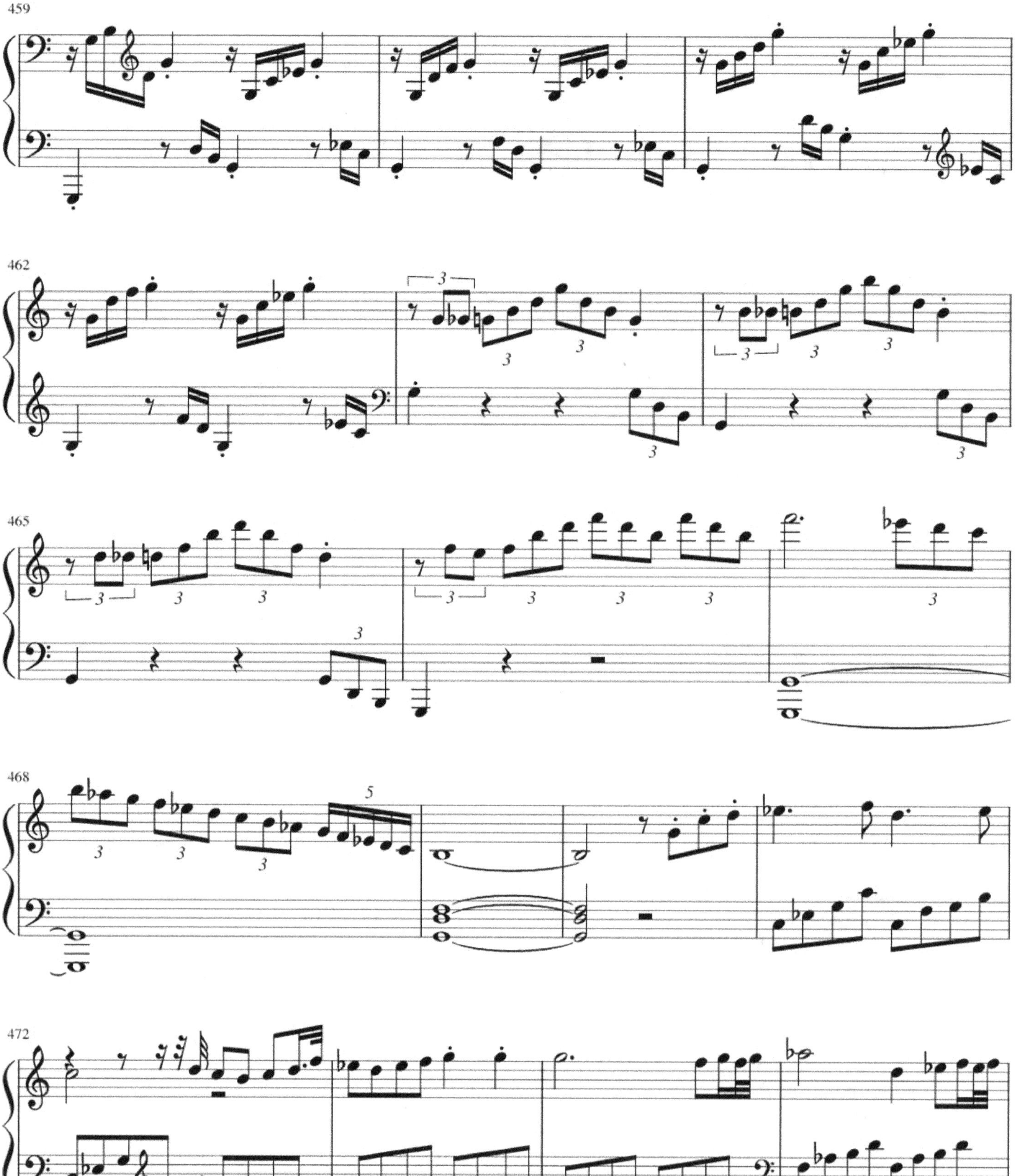
459
462
465
468
472

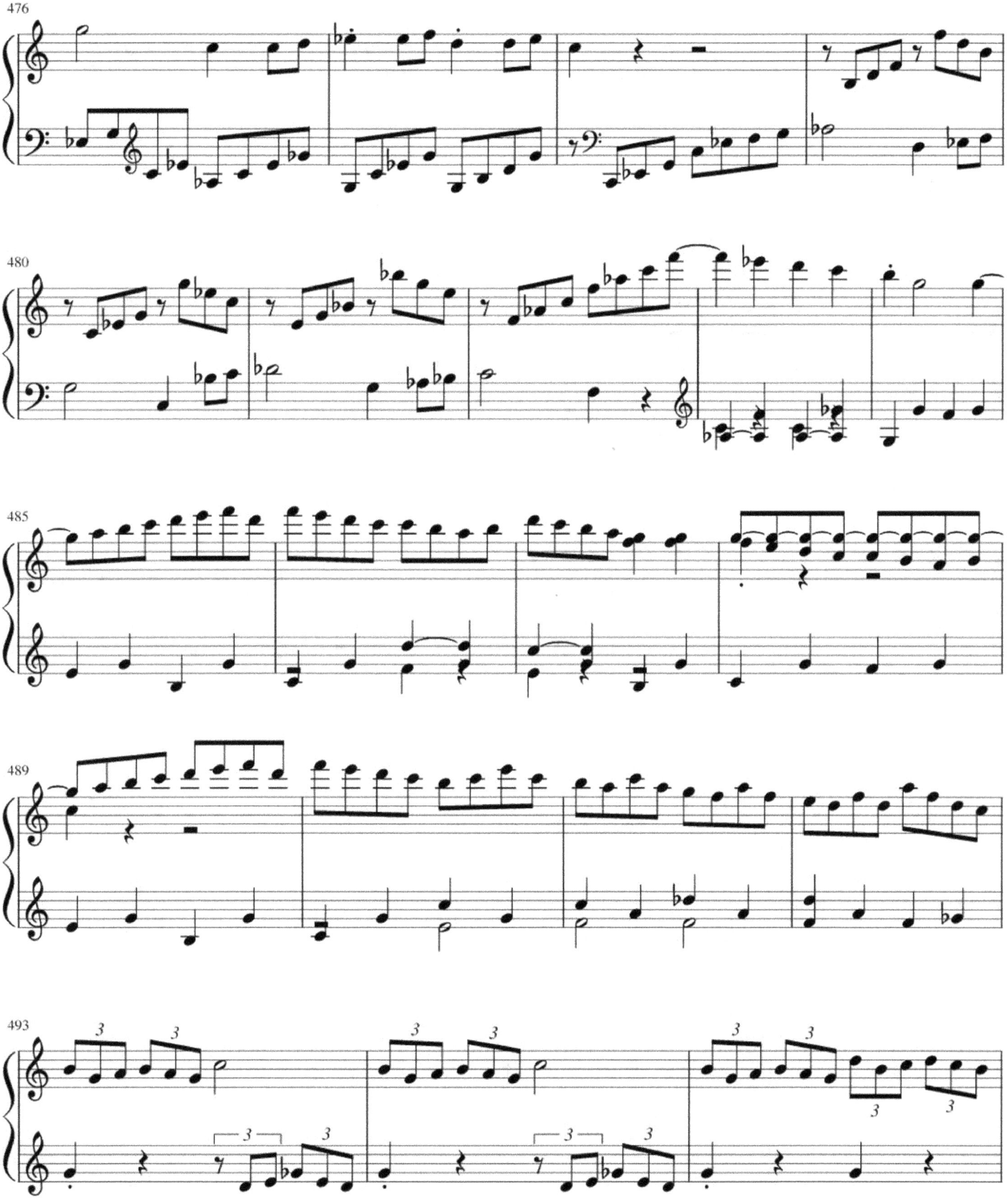
476
480
485
489
493

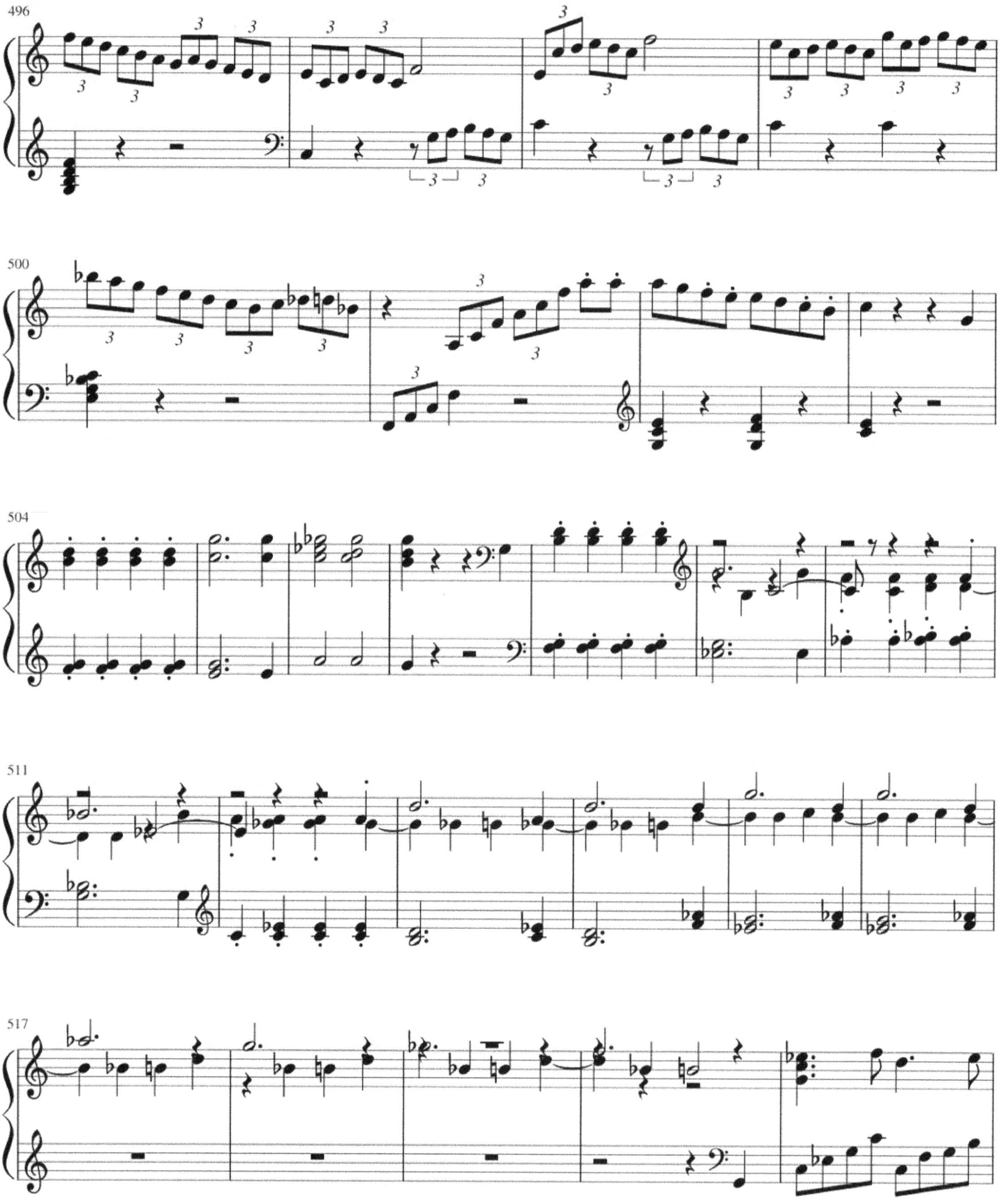
496
500
504
511
517

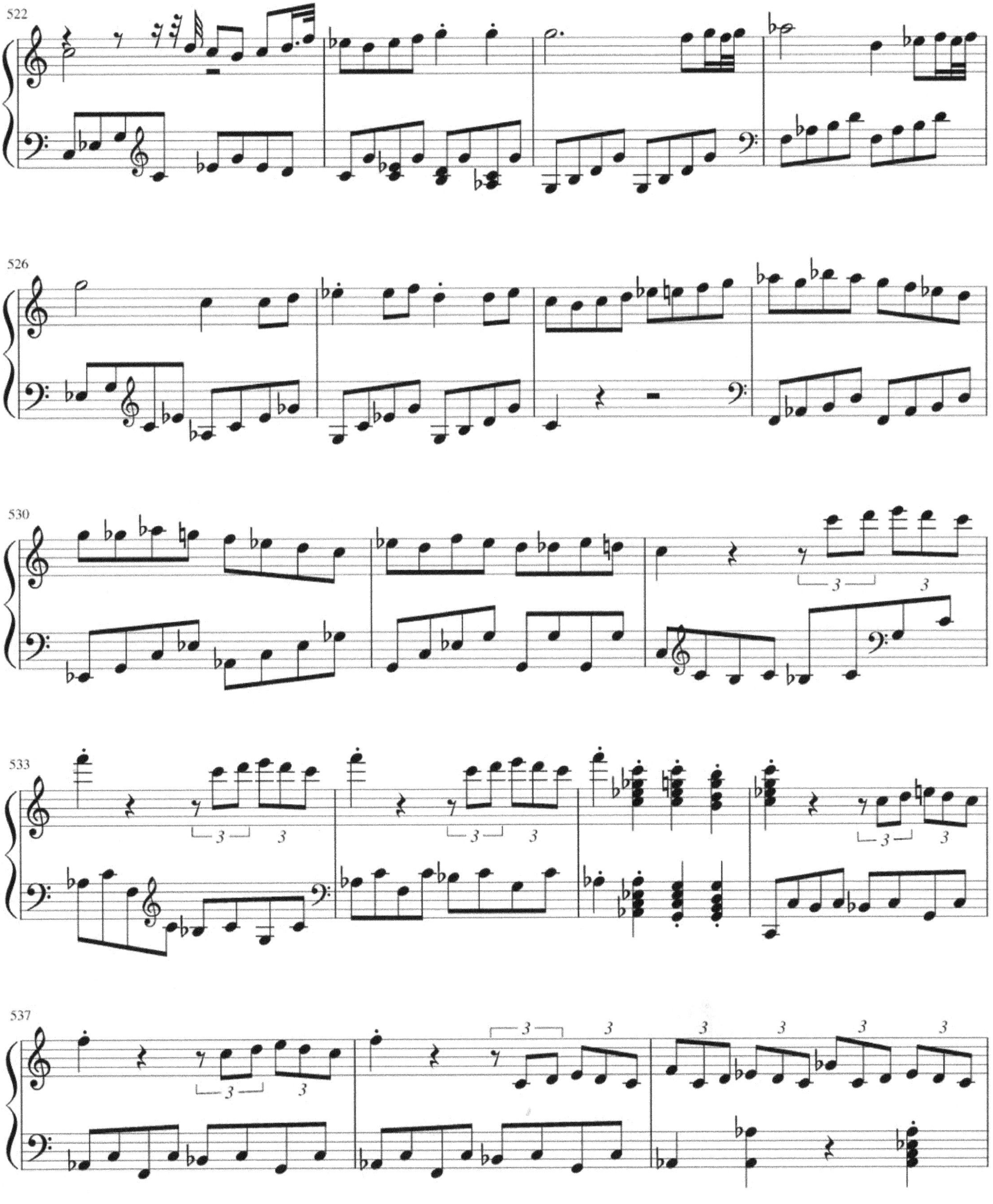
522
526
530
533
537

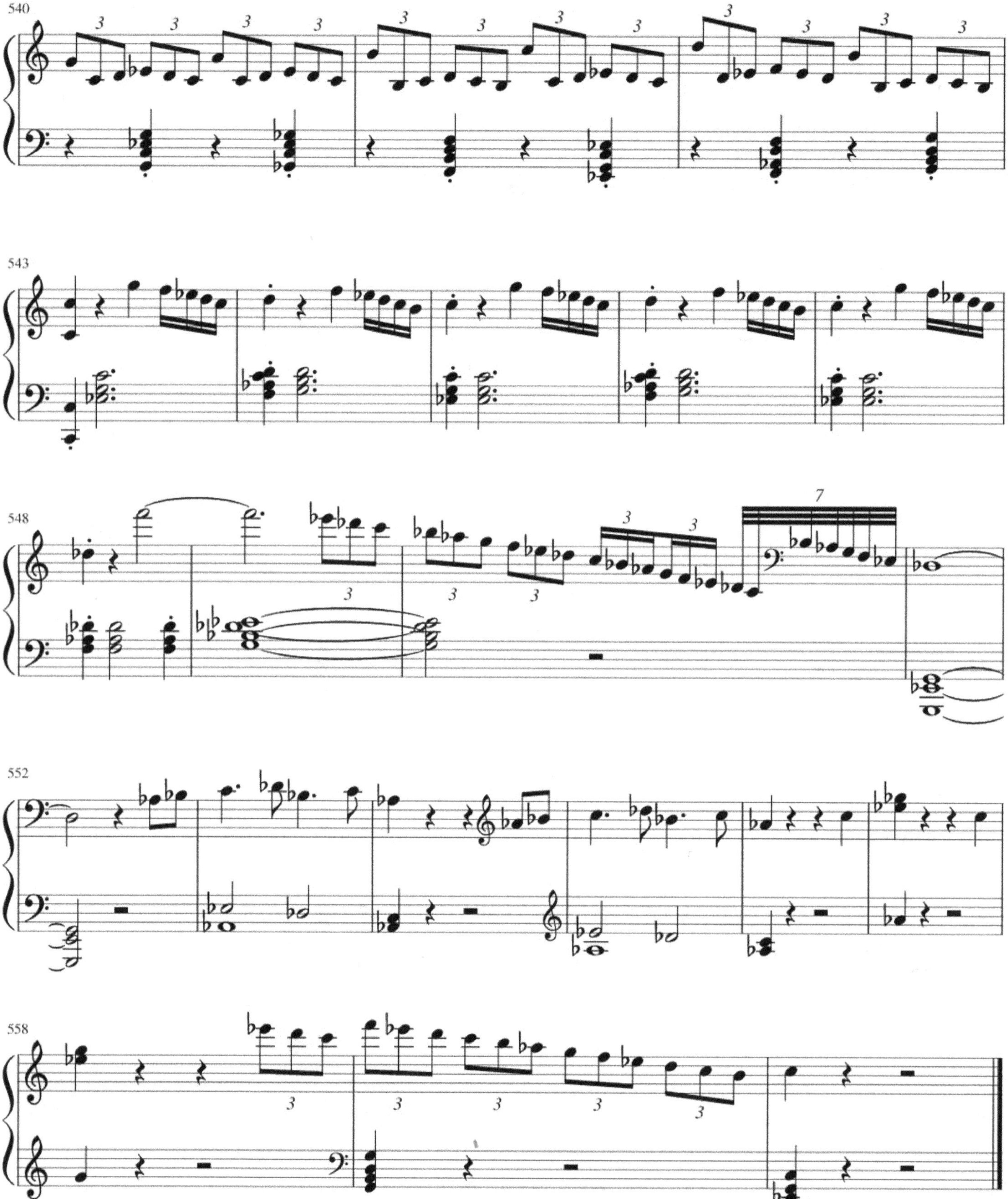
540
543
548
552
558

Moonlight Sonata
Sonata No 14, Opus 27, No 2

Ludwig Van Beethoven

Adagio Sostenuto.

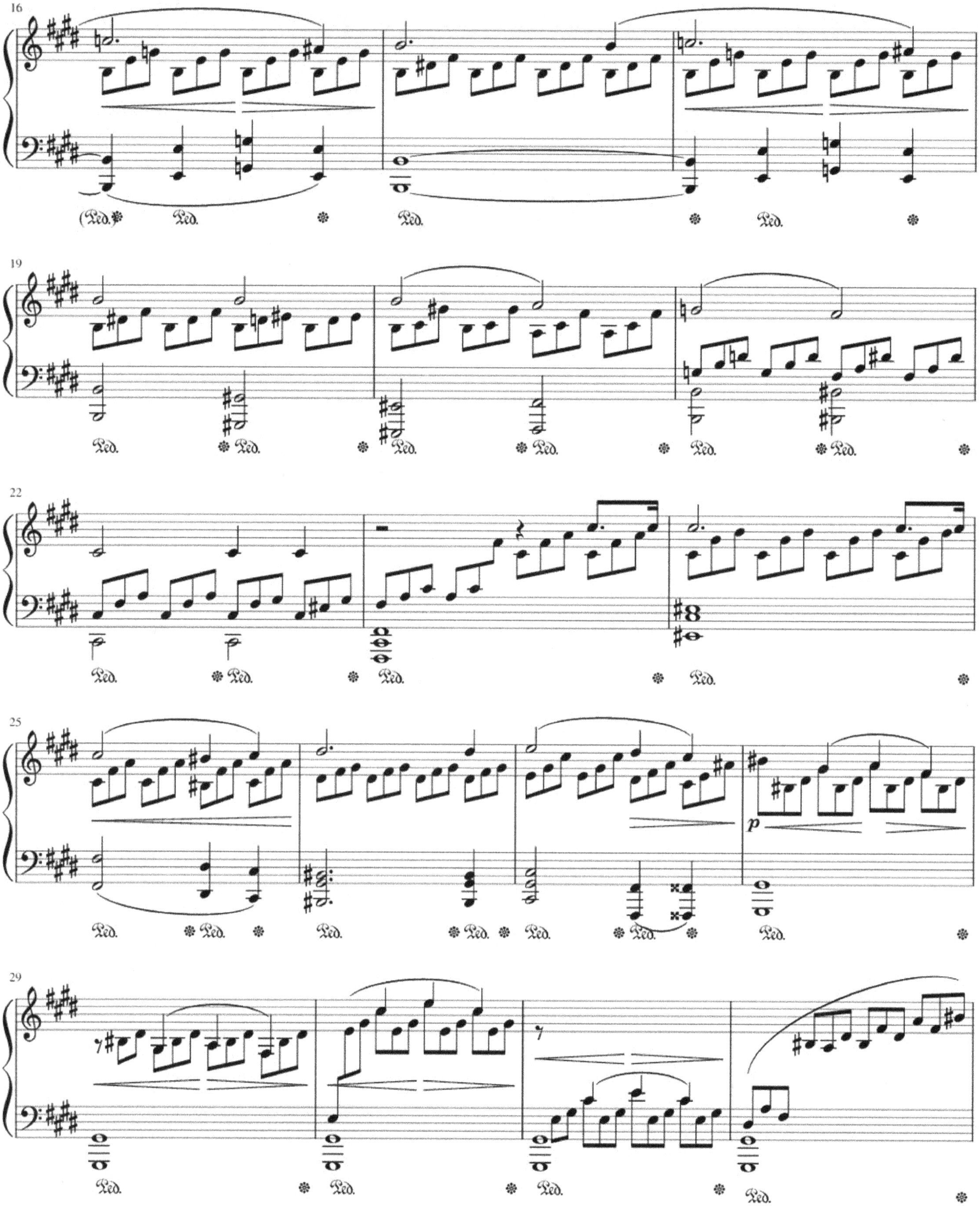
16
19
22
25
29

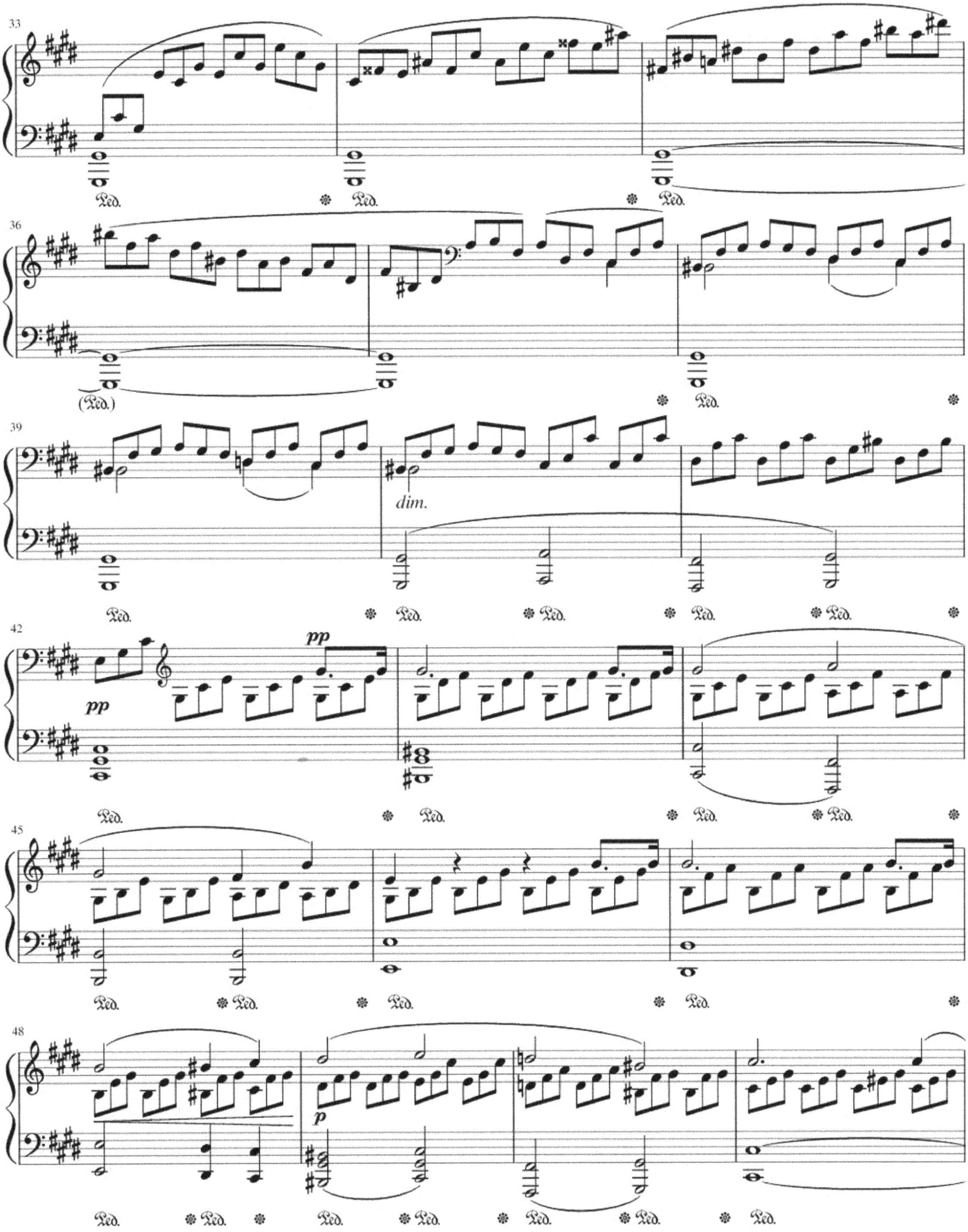
33
36
(Ped.)
39
dim.
42
pp
pp
45
48
p
Ped.

52
(Ped.) Ped. Ped. Ped.
55
Ped. Ped. Ped. Ped. Ped. Ped.
58
p
pp
Ped. Ped. Ped. Ped. Ped.
61
Ped. Ped. Ped.
64
dim.
Ped. Ped. Ped.

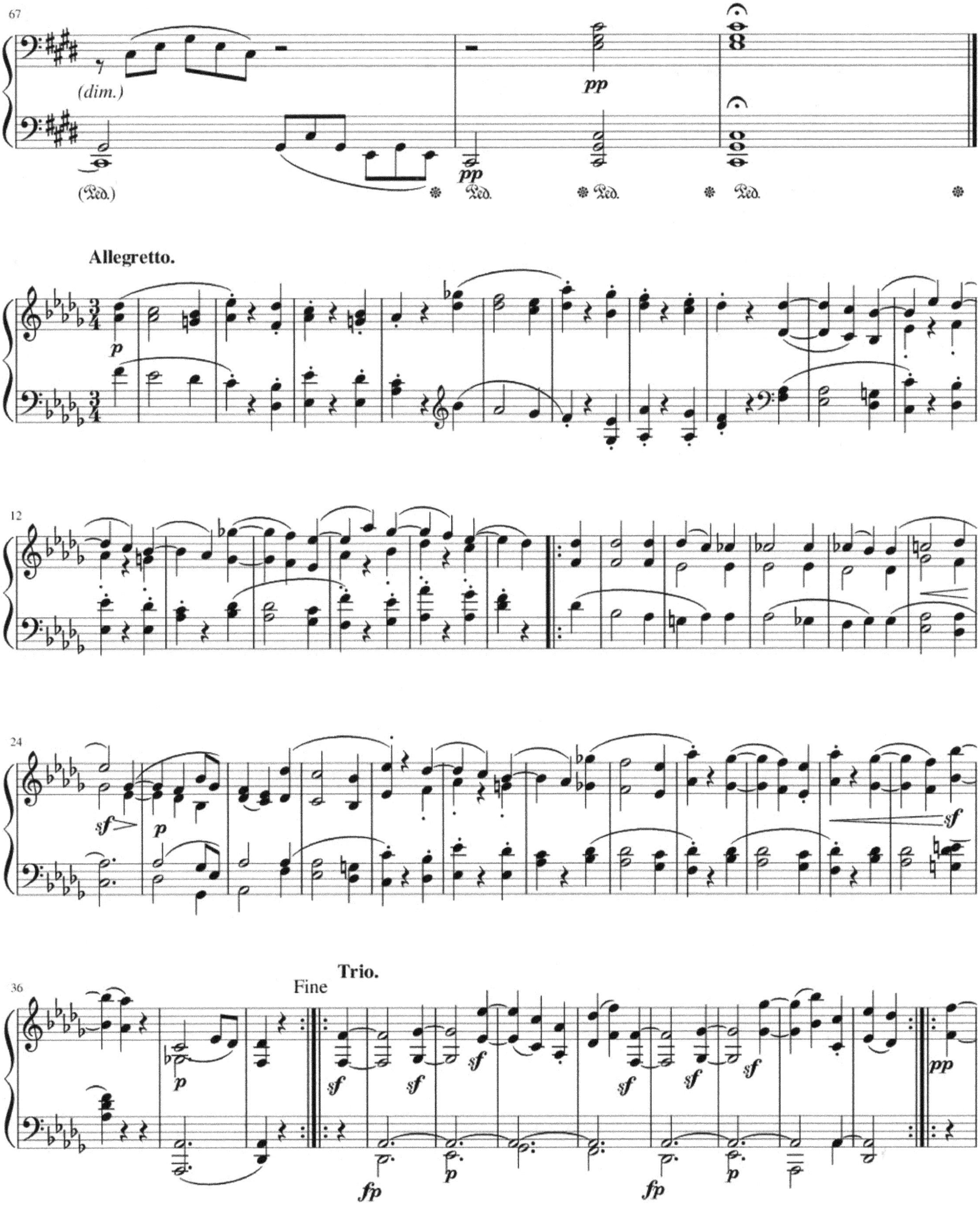
67
(dim.)
pp
(Ped.)
Ped.
Allegretto.
p
12
24
sf
36
Fine
Trio.
fp
pp

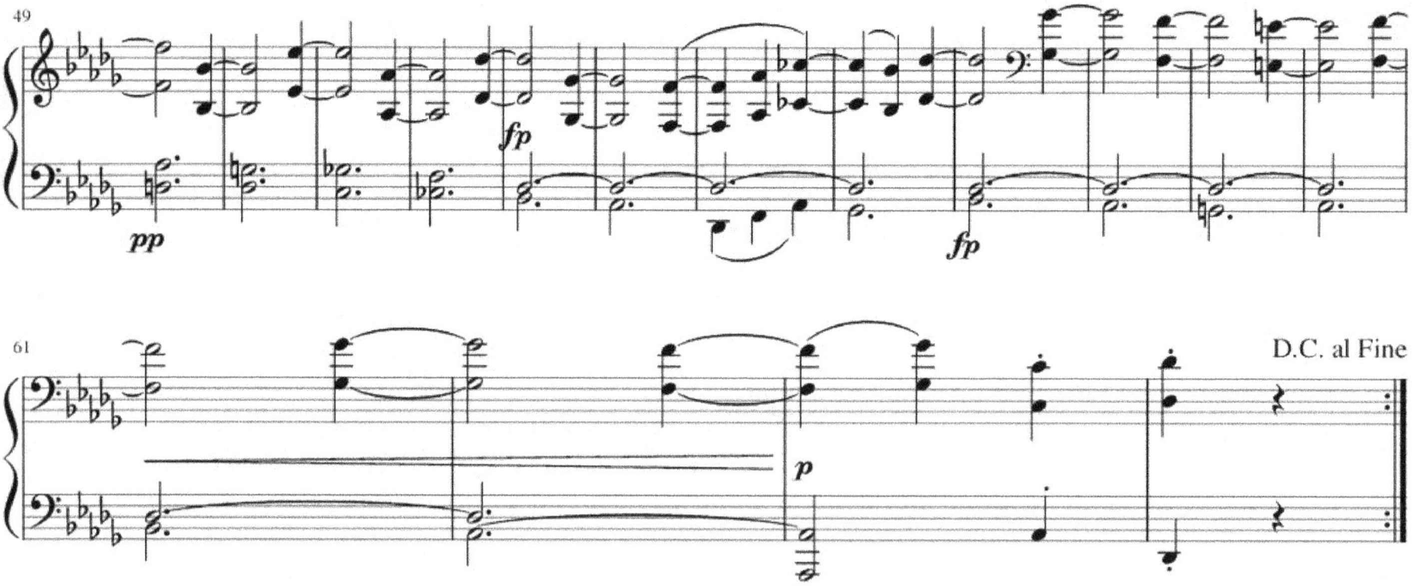
49
pp
fp
fp
61
D.C. al Fine
p

Presto Agitato

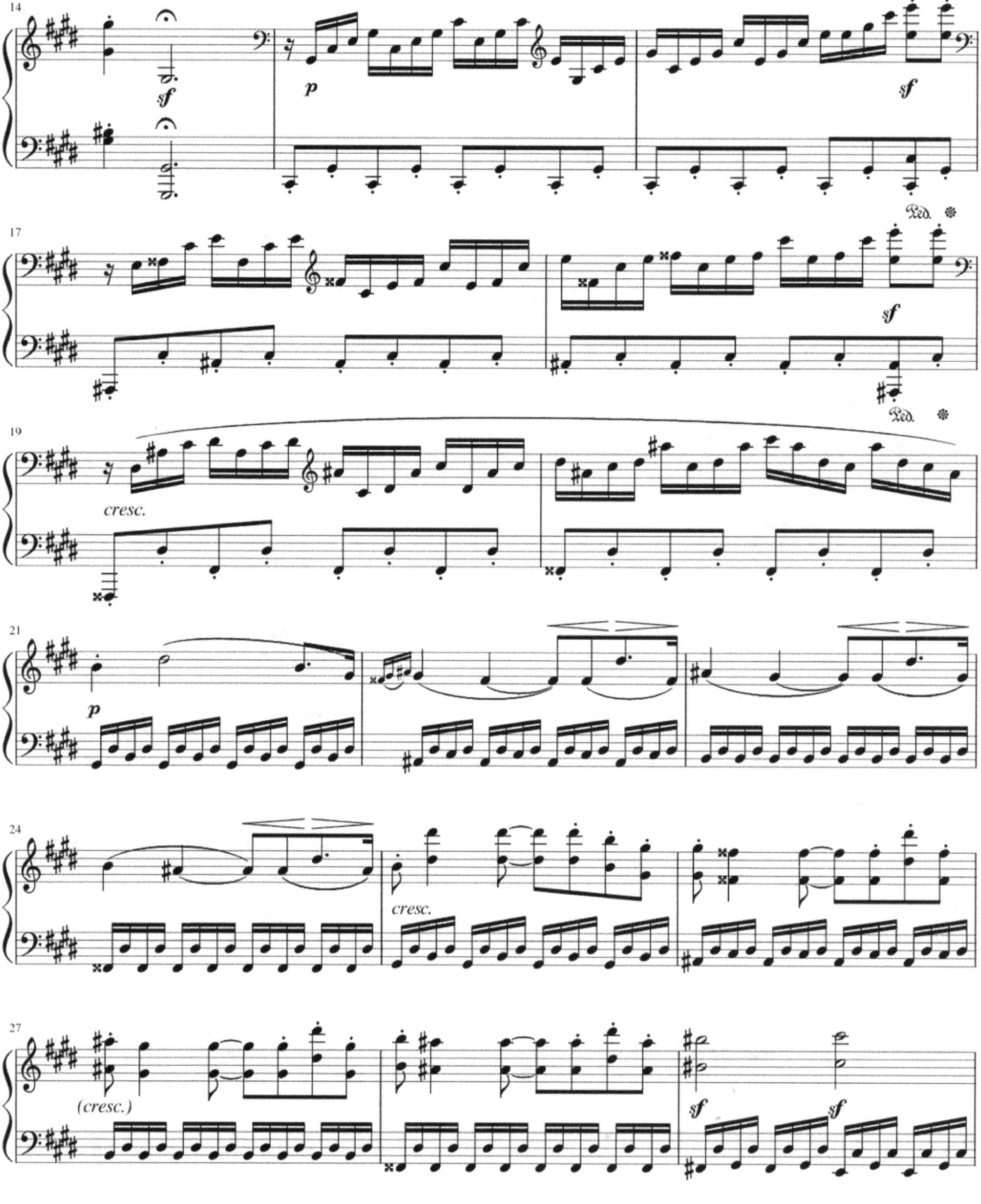
14
sf
p
sf
Ped.
17
sf
Ped.
19
cresc.
21
p
24
cresc.
27
(cresc.)
sf
sf

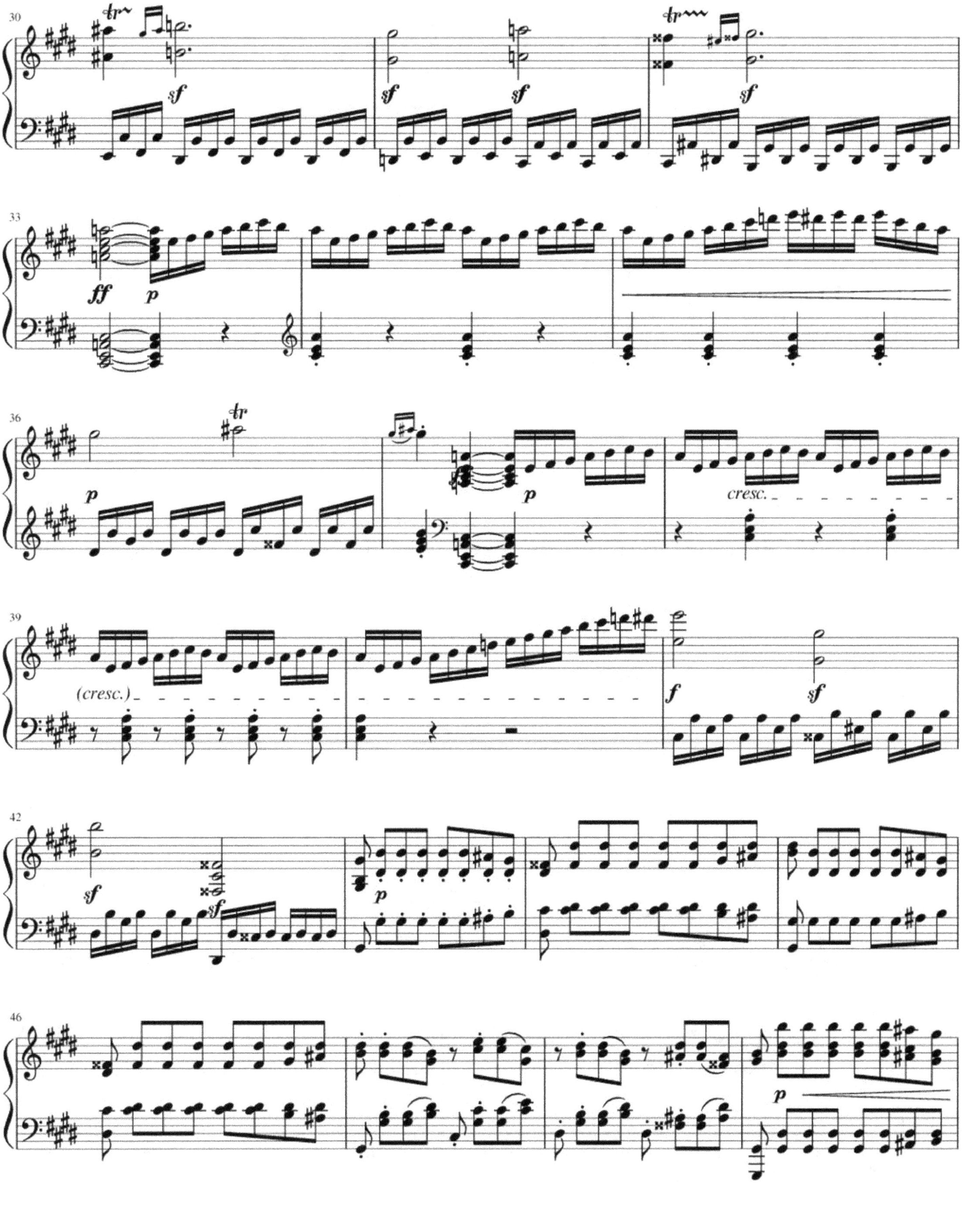
30
tr
sf
tr
33
ff
p
36
tr
p
cresc.
39
(cresc.)
f
sf
42
sf
p
46
p

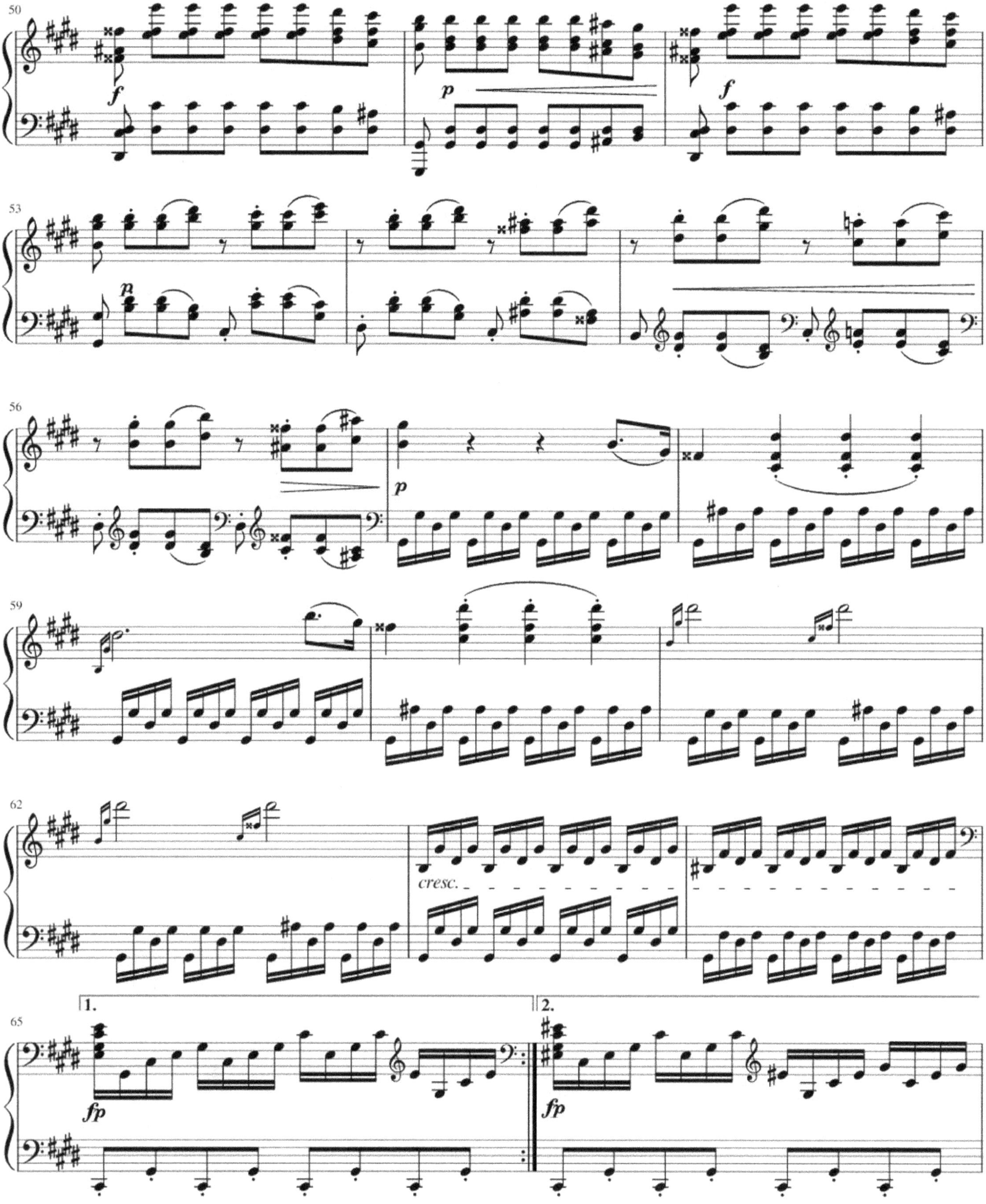
50
f
p
f
53
p
56
p
59
62
cresc.
1.
2.
65
fp
fp

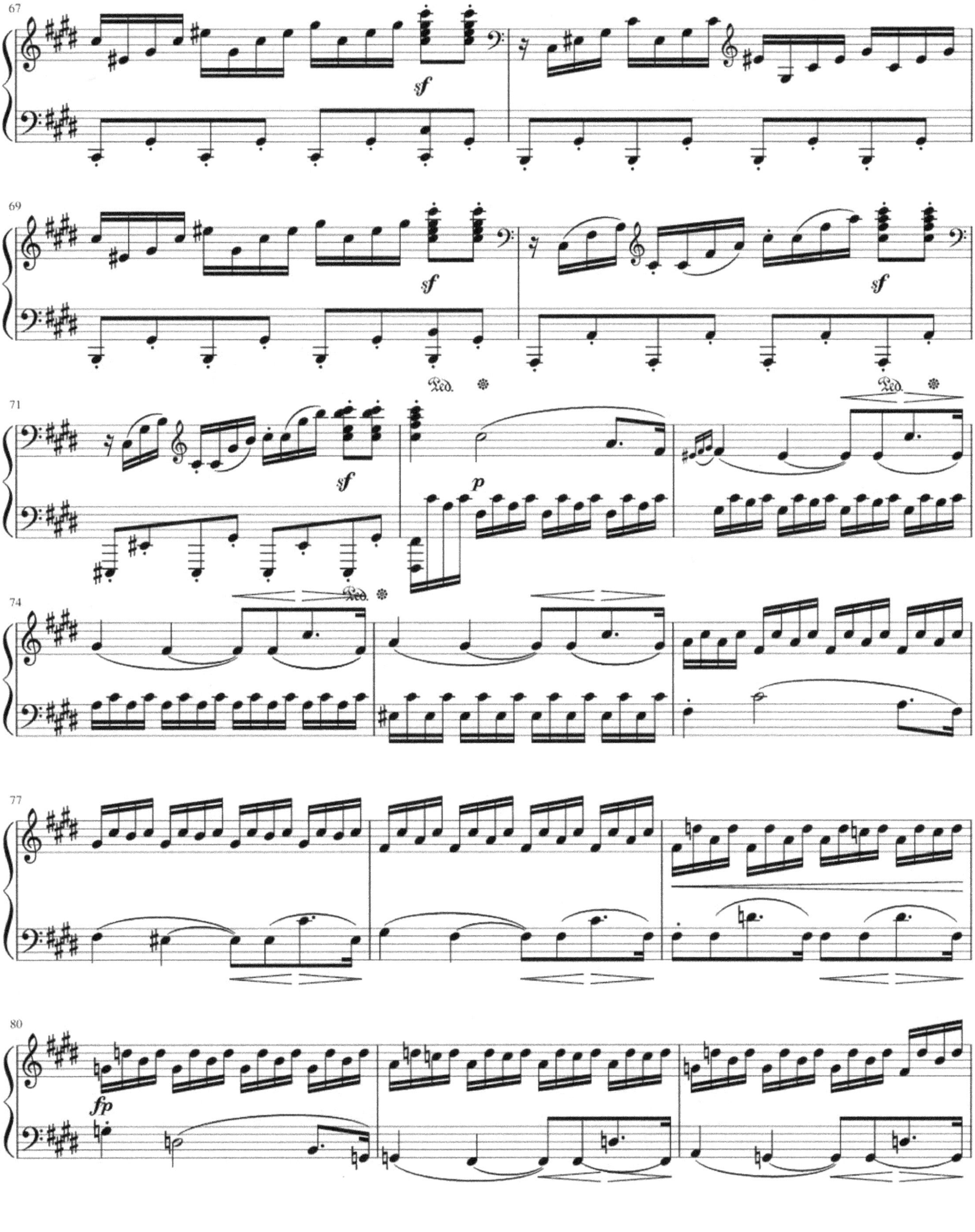
67
sf
69
sf
sf
Ped.
Ped.
71
sf
p
74
Ped.
77
80
fp

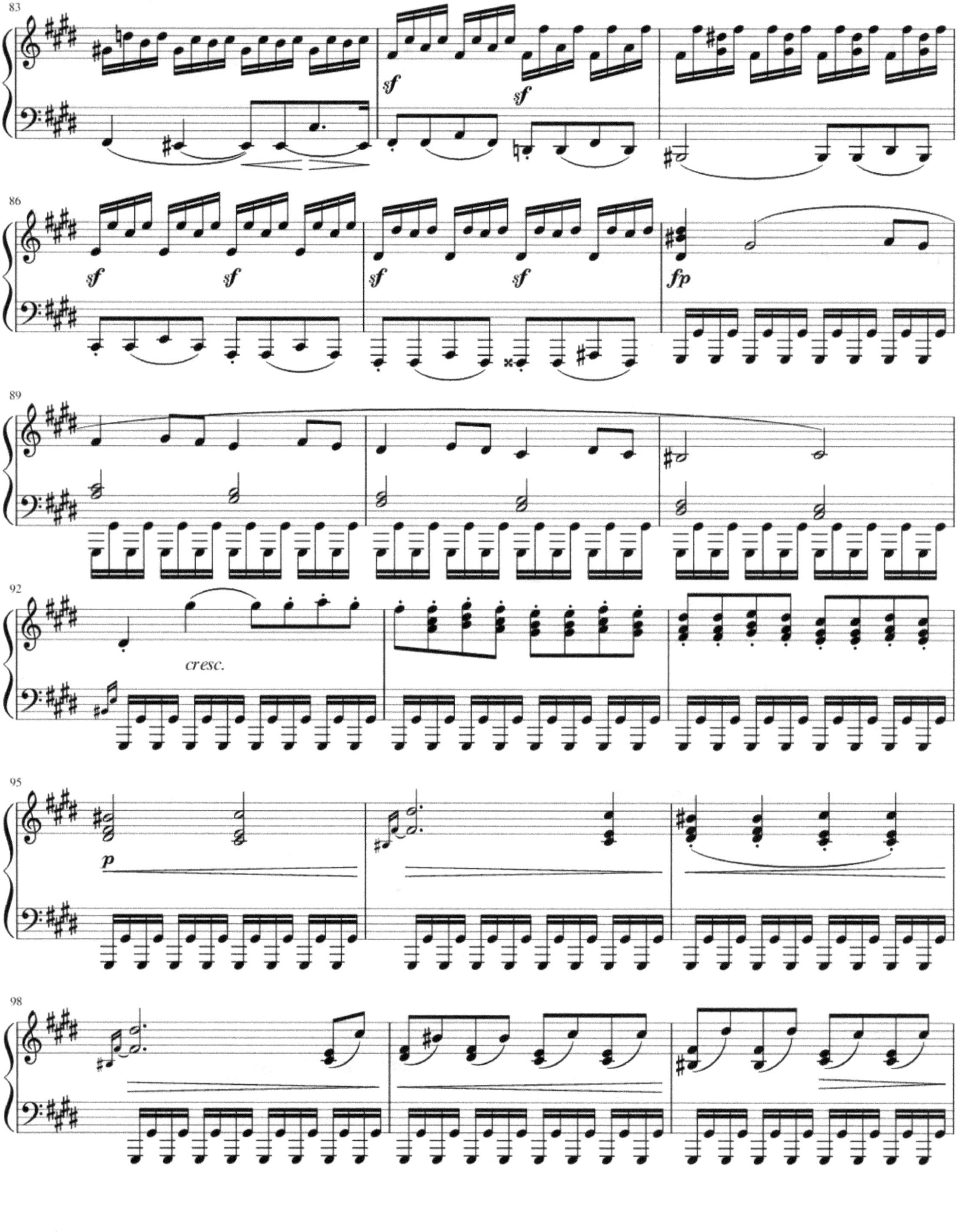
83
sf
sf
86
sf
sf
sf
sf
fp
89
92
cresc.
95
p
98

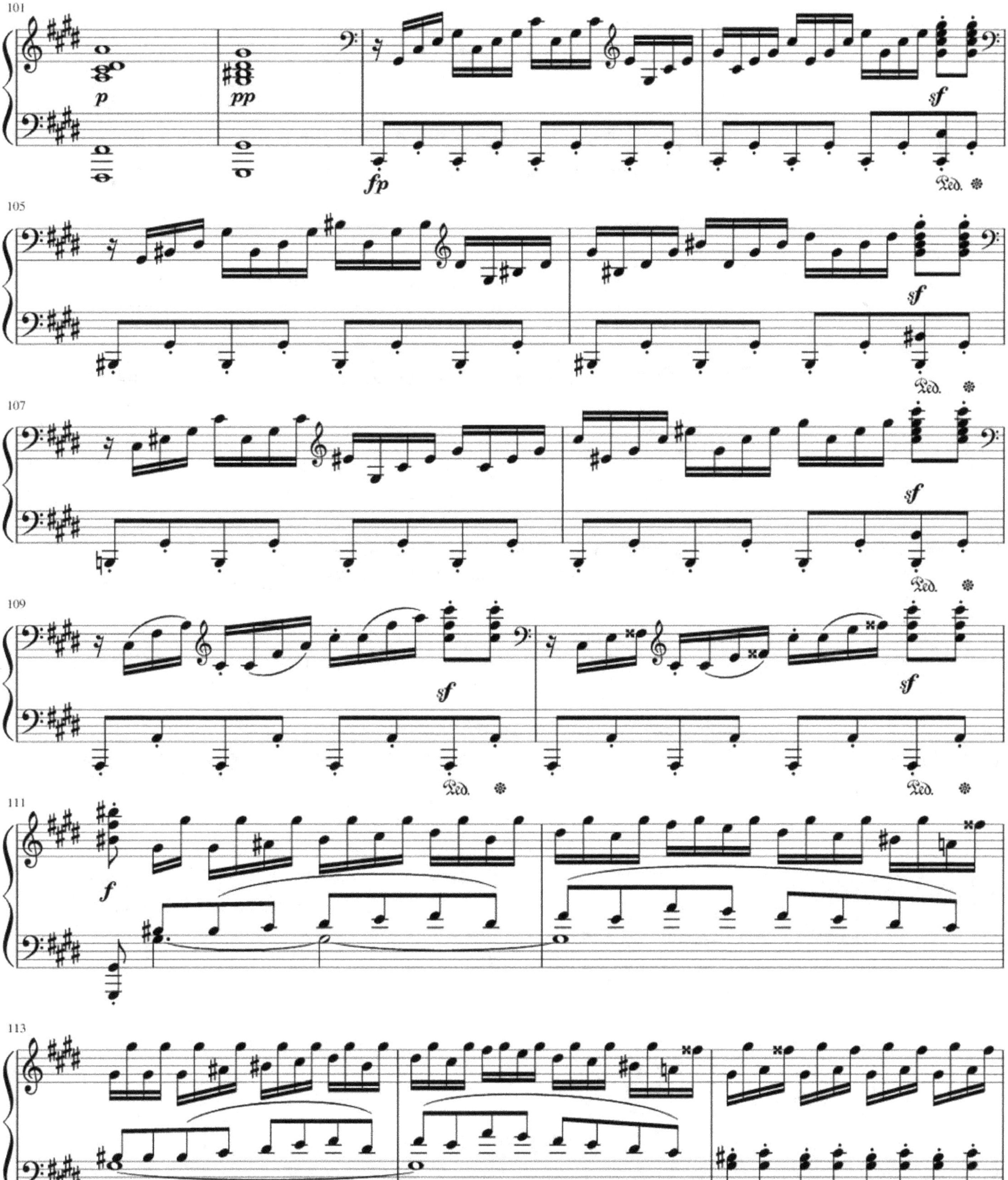
101
p
pp
fp
sf
Ped.
105
sf
Ped.
107
sf
Ped.
109
sf
Ped.
sf
Ped.
111
f
113

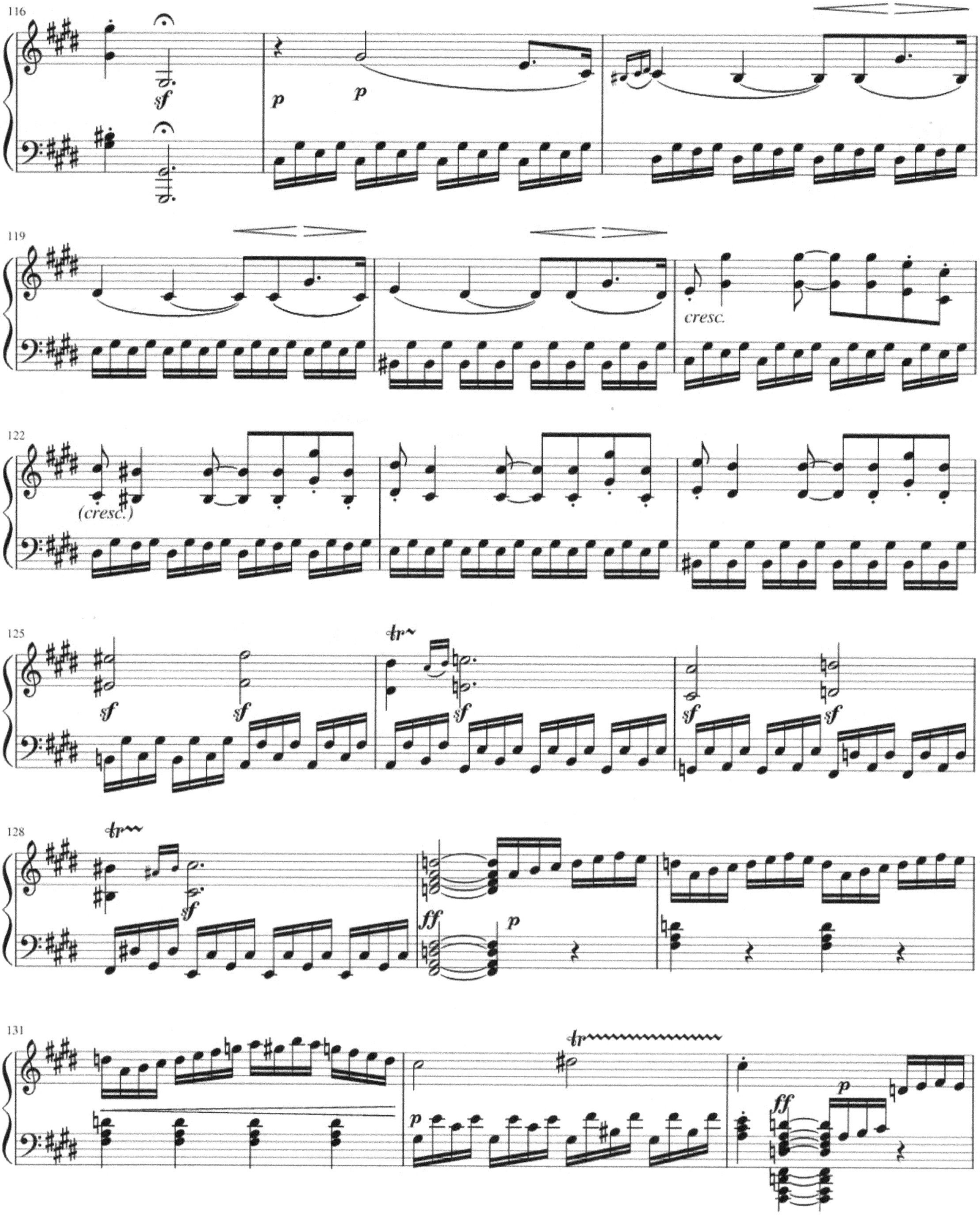
cresc.
(cresc.)

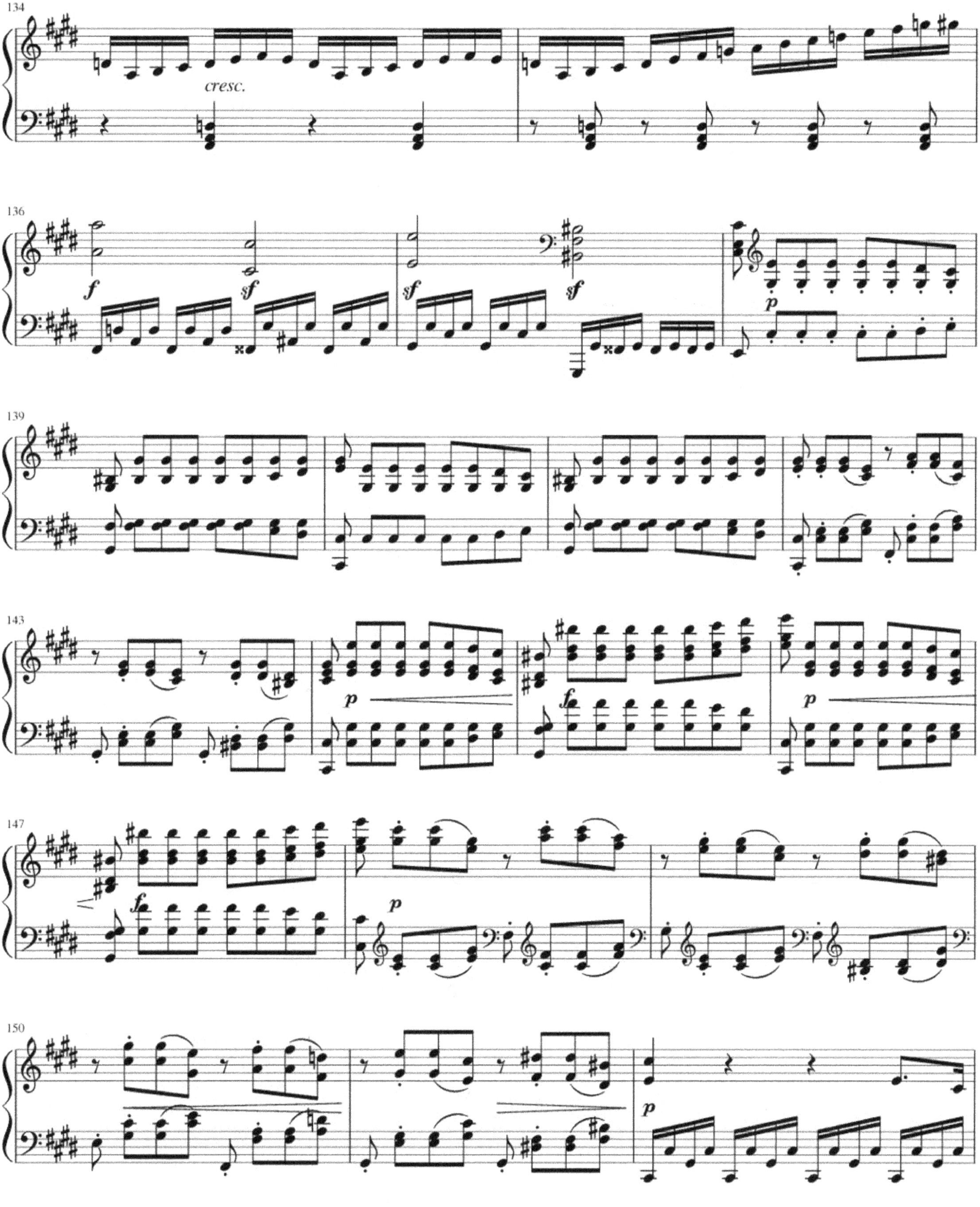
134
cresc.
136
f
sf
sf
sf
p
139
143
p
f
p
147
f
p
150
p

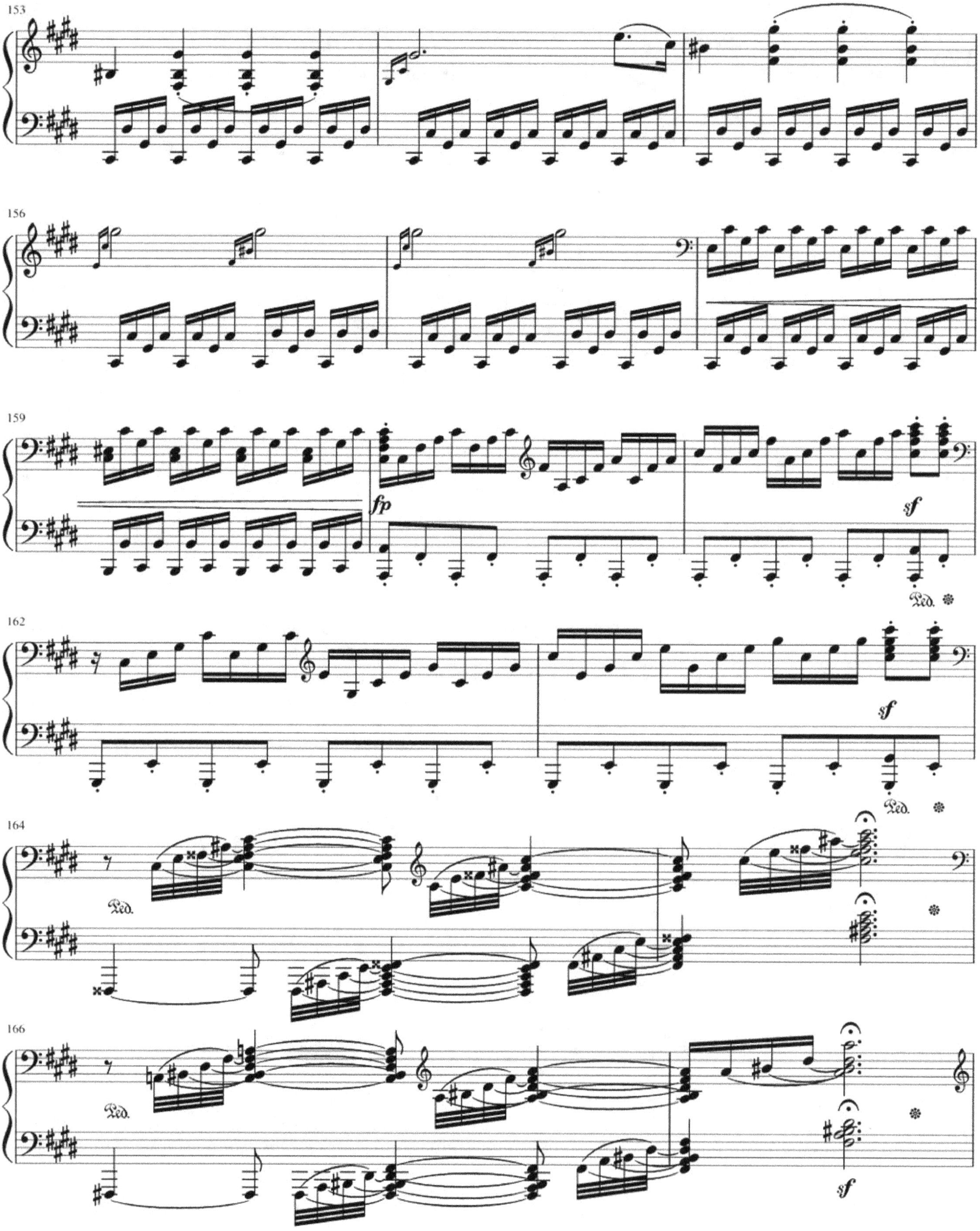
153
156
159
fp
sf
Ped.
162
sf
Ped.
164
Ped.
166
Ped.
sf

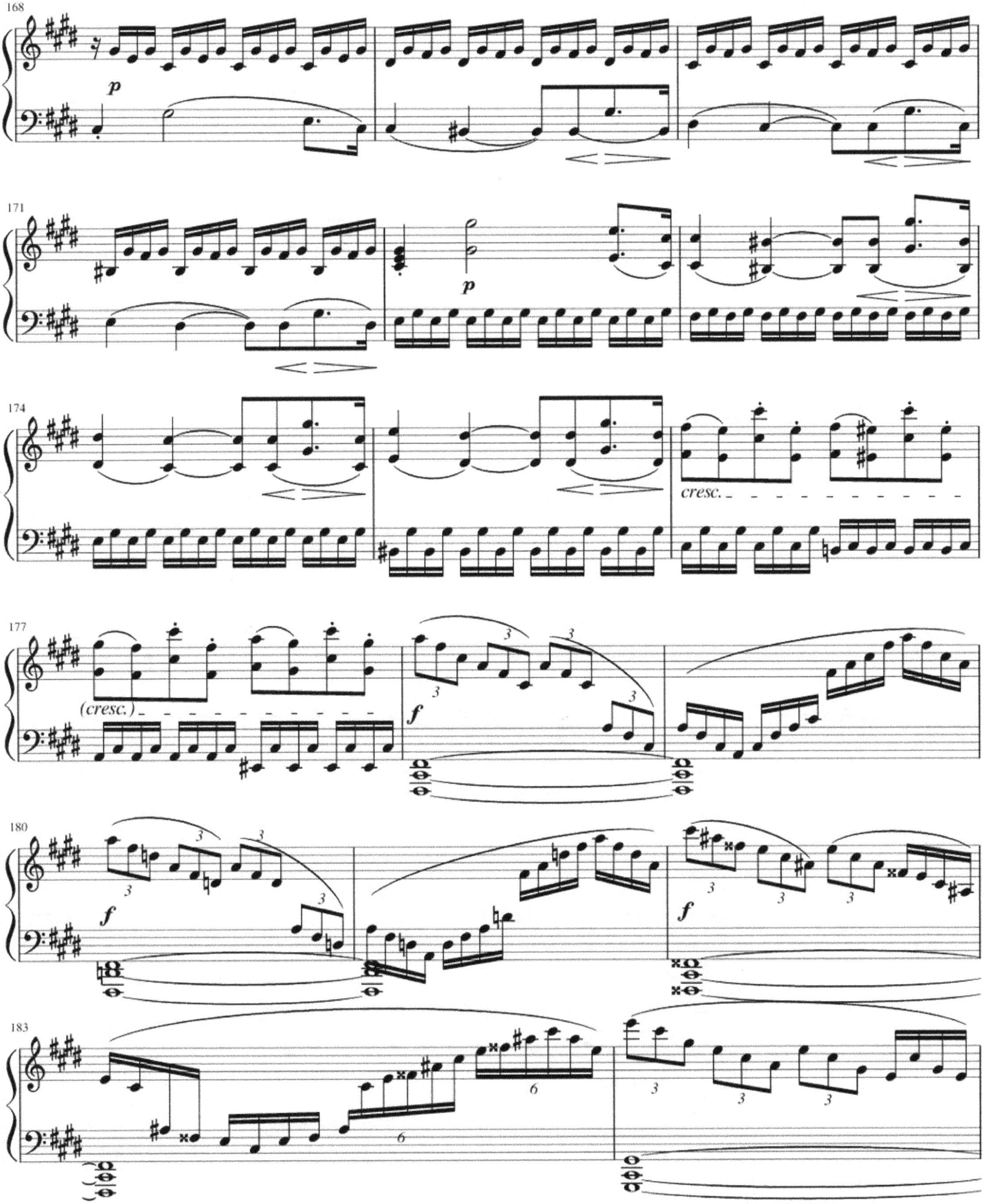
168
p
171
p
174
cresc.
177
(cresc.)
f
180
f
f
183
6
6

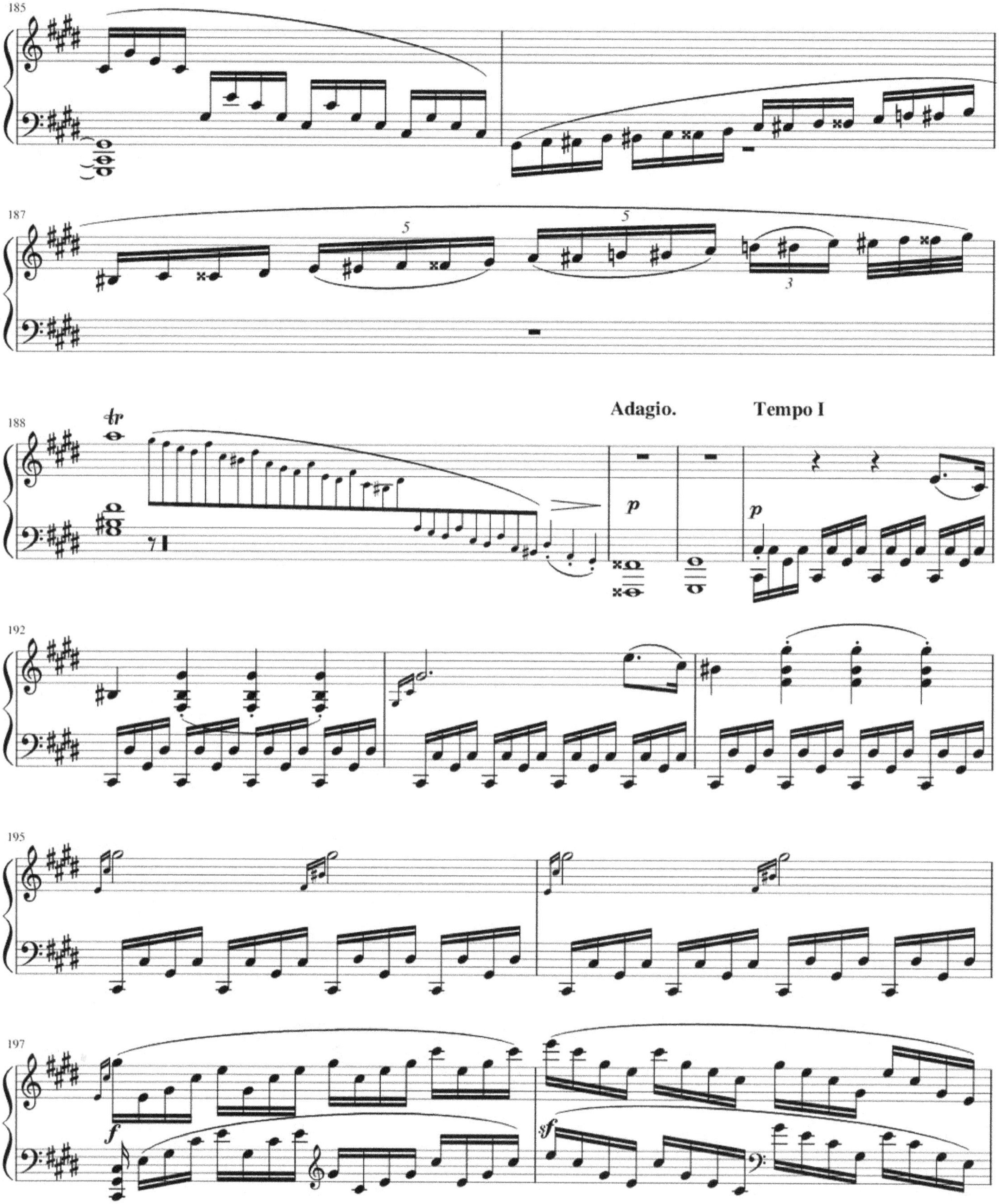
185
187
5
5
3
188
tr
Adagio.
Tempo I
p
p
192
195
197
f
sf

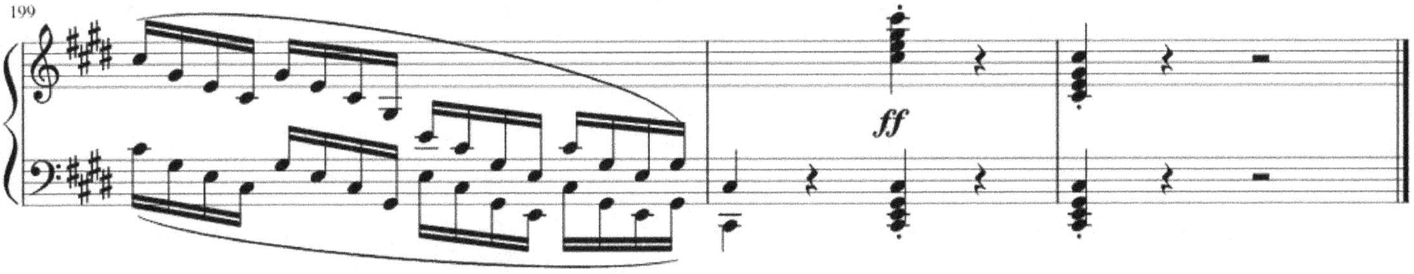
199
ff

Flight of the Bumblebee

Rimsky-Korsakov

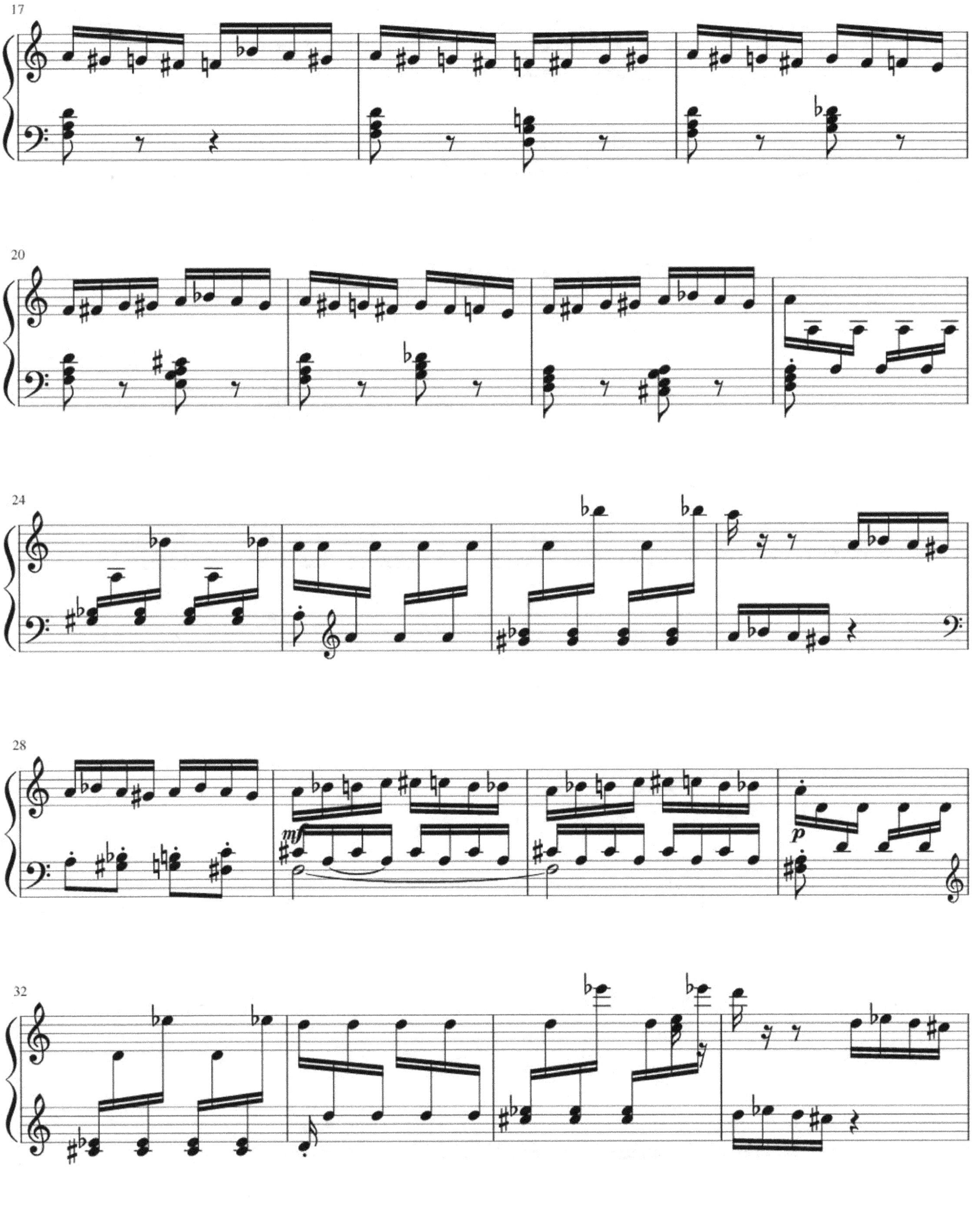
17
20
24
28
mf
p
32

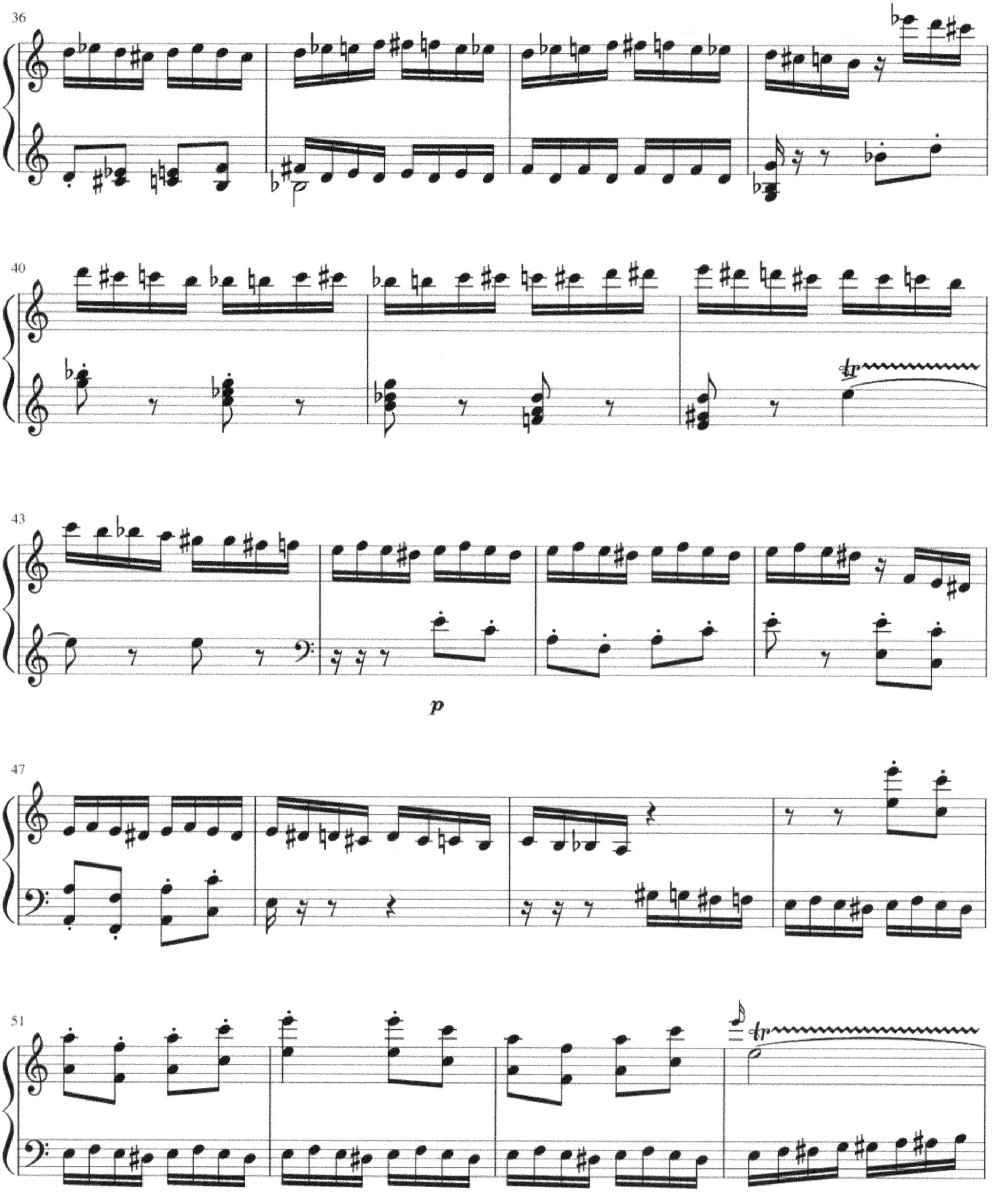
36
40
tr
43
p
47
51
tr

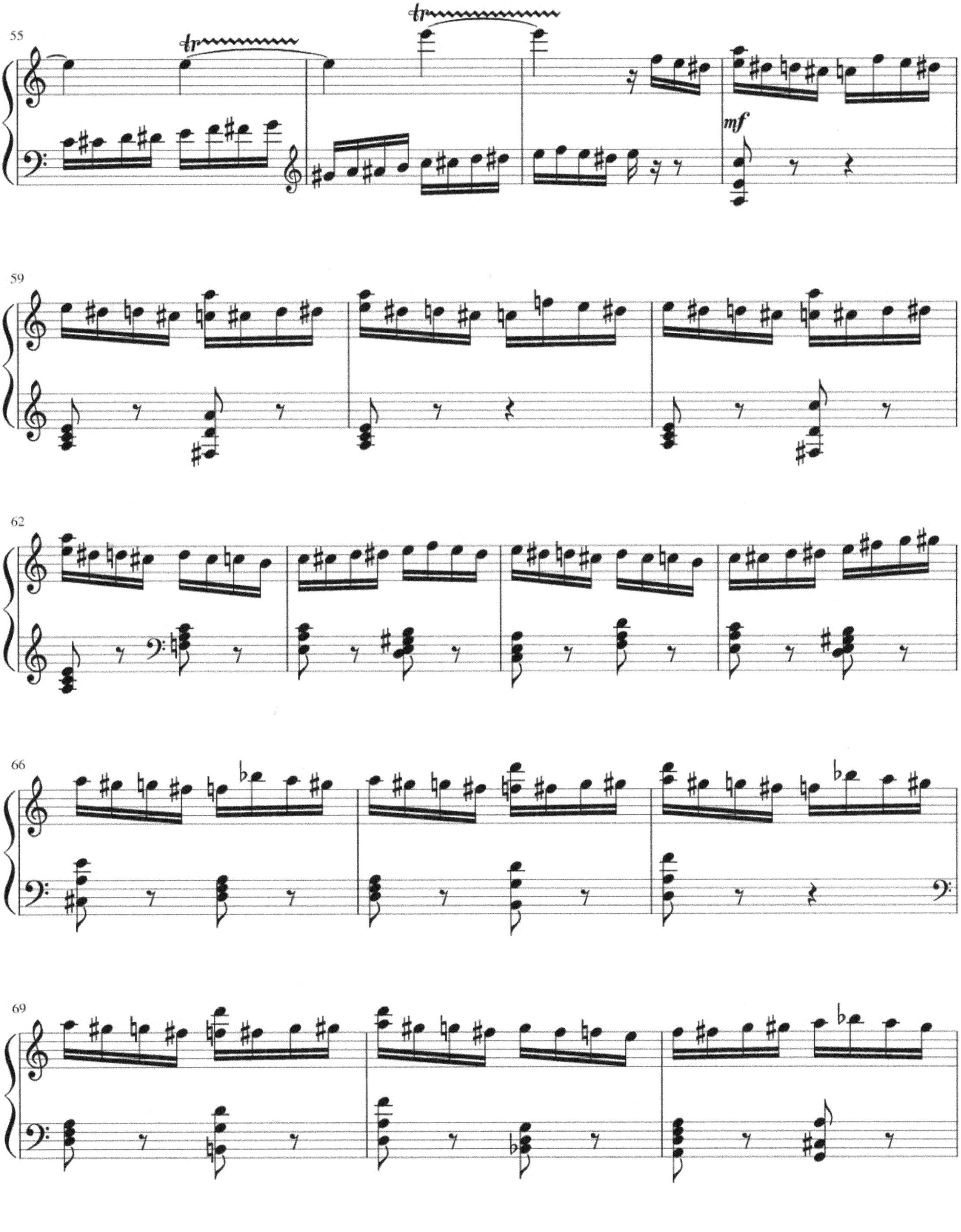
55
tr
tr
mf
59
62
66
69

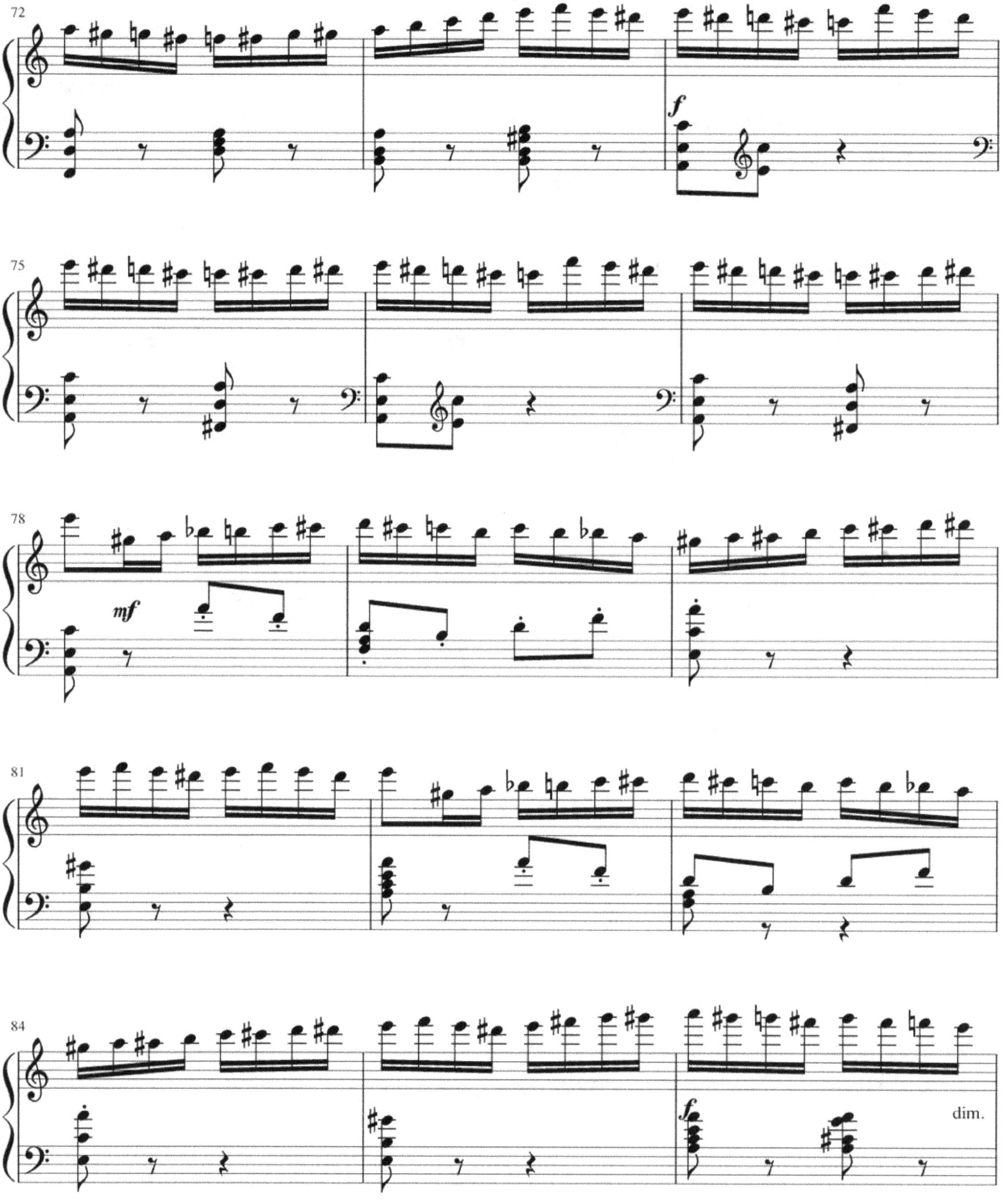
72
f
75
78
mf
81
84
f
dim.

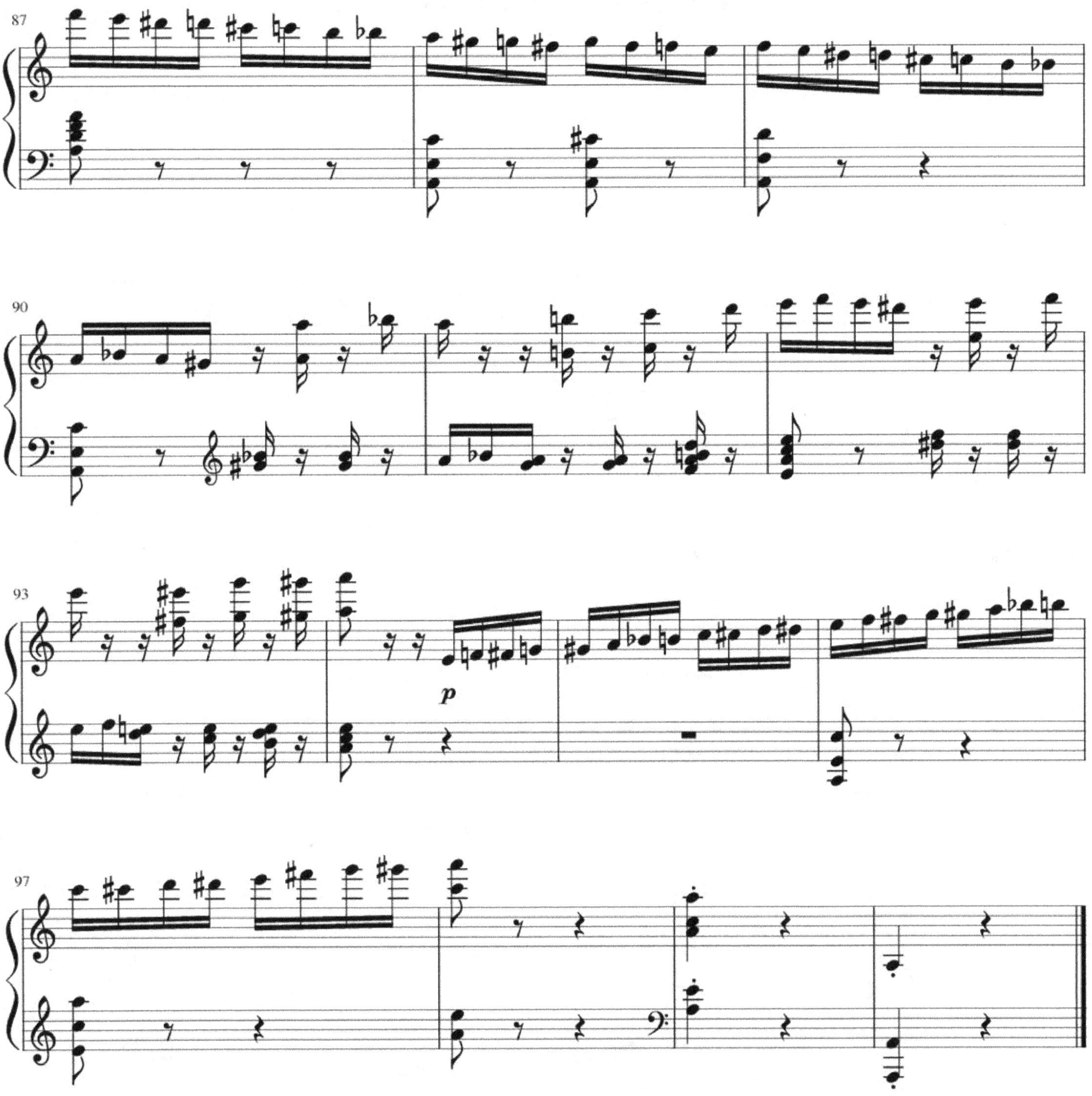
87
90
93
p
97

Prelude in D Minor

Opus 23, No 3

Sergei Rachmaninoff

Tempo di minuetto. (♩ = 66)

18
p
mf
21
f
mf
Un poco più mosso.
24
mf
27
f
p
30
cresc.
33
f
marcato
ff

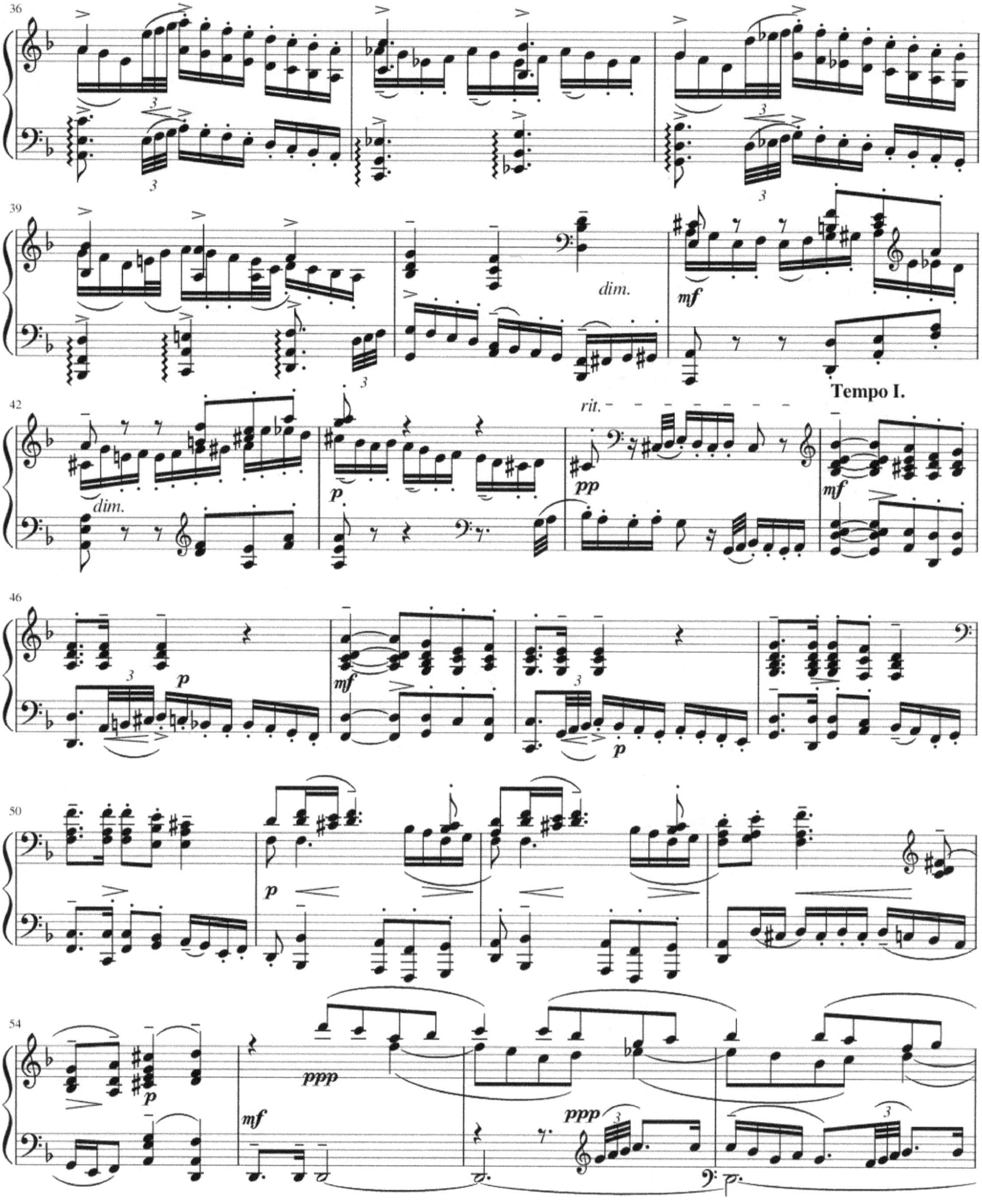

dim.
mf
rit.
Tempo I.
dim.
p
pp
mf
p
mf
p
p
p
p
ppp
mf
ppp

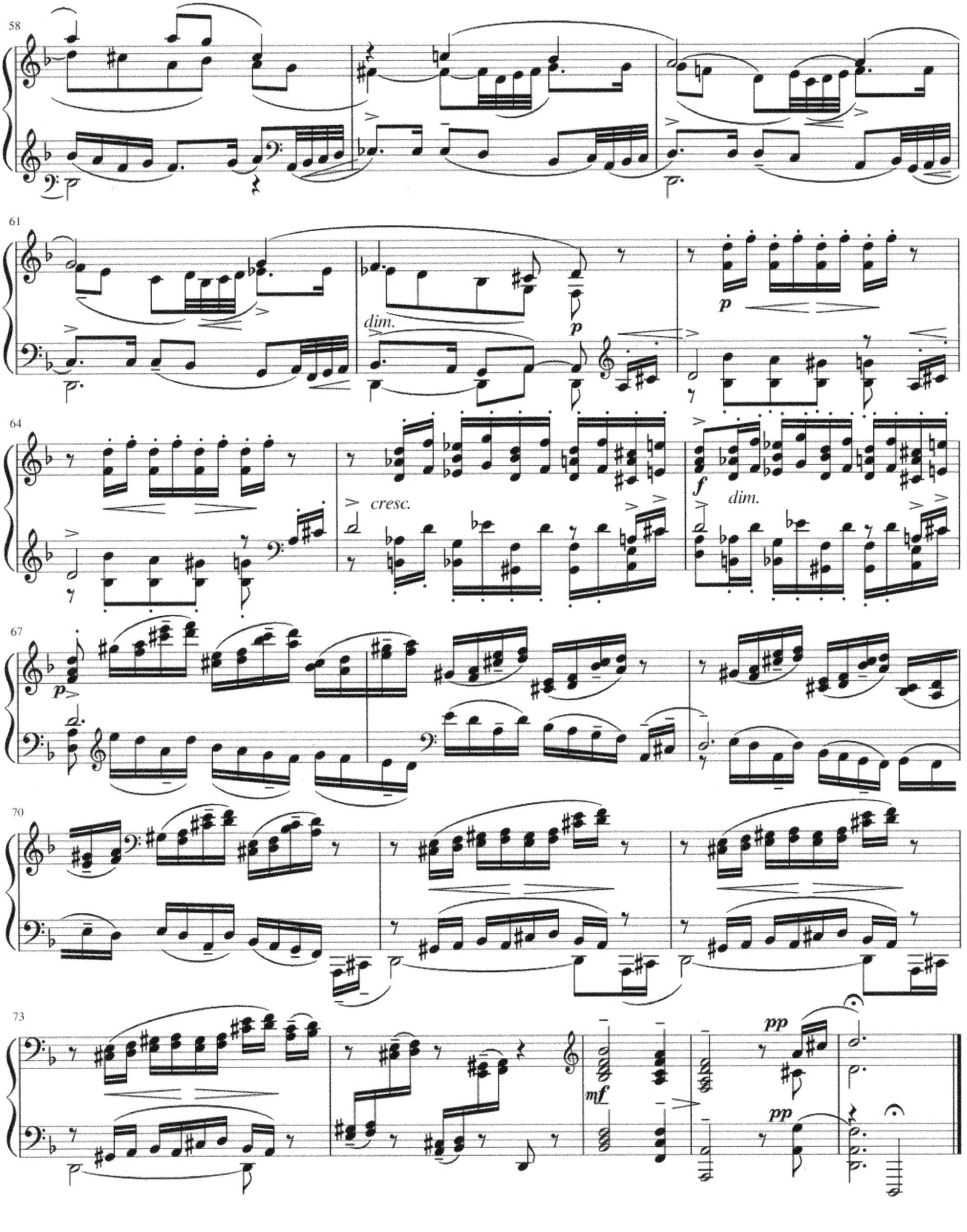
58
61
dim.
p
p
64
cresc.
f
dim.
67
p
70
73
mf
pp
pp